Introduction

Preparation for Christmas starts months before the holiday. Gift-giving ideas are collected and supplies are sought after. But what about the rest of the year? For special occasions, birthday, graduation, showers, weddings, and anniversaries, our "brainstorms" get a little dull. It doesn't necessarily have to be Christmas to make that special quilt, gift, or gift basket. Hopefully, this book will inspire you to make every holiday special.

Quick-cutting and piecing techniques are used in this book whenever possible. The use of a rotary cutter, mat board, and plastic template ruler is required for most of the projects. Quick and easy projects, as well as more advanced projects, are included. There are a total of 42 projects and 12 recipes. All of the recipes are family favorites, simple to make, and are stored easily for inclusion in a gift basket. So, don't wait for Christmas to cook or sew up some creative gift ideas, start now! (By the way, once in a while you deserve a gift too!)

Acknowledgements

Special thanks to my Mom, Frasha Evanoff, Judy Walker, Cindy Boucher, Sue Neumaier, Beth Gray, Gaye Mason, and Meg Walters, for giving me the extra help and incentive when I was so hurried by deadlines. A special thank-you goes to Carol Mellors for working out all the fine details on my quilt graphics. A special thanks to Trish Taft Johnson for coming up with great illustrations at the last minute. Also, much gratitude goes to my uncle, Sam Zatkoff, for hand carving all of the wonderful Santas pictured throughout this book. (Not for sale!!) Lastly, a heart felt thank you to Nina and Fred Flack, for opening their shop, Fancies, in Erie, Pennsylvania, to me for my photography session.

Credits

My sewing group: Frasha Evanoff, Judy Walker, Beth Gray,
Cindy Boucher, Sue Neumaier
Judy Walker - designer of Judy's table runner
Tom Carter - TLC Photography
Trish Taft Johnson - Illustrations
Boyd Press - Printing

ISBN: 0-9630473-0-2
Manufactured in the United States of America
First printing, 1991

The Quilted Cottage
Susan Bartlett
527 Cunningham Drive
Erie, Pennsylvania 16511

TABLE OF CONTENTS

Recipes

GENERAL INSTRUCTIONS

✱ Quick-cutting strips of fabric: Place fabric on flat surface. Fold fabric in half, selvage to selvage. Fold fabric in half again, fold to selvage. There are now four thicknesses. Now straighten the raw edges with a right-angle triangle, having one edge of triangle even with the folded edge of fabric. With rotary cutter trim the raw edges. You are now ready to cut your strips. (After cutting four strips you may want to straighten your fabric edge again.)

✱ Seams: Sew exactly 1/4" seams unless otherwise noted.

✱ Chain stitching: Do not break off your thread between stitching pieces. Simply butt the next piece to be sewn directly behind the piece being stitched. Sew as many pieces at a time as you can. When finished, clip the sections apart.

✱ Butting seams: Usually if you have pressed your work accurately, the seams, when lined up, will butt together. That is, the two seams should have their allowances pressed in opposite directions.

✱ Matching up points: Use a straight pin to line up the points to be sewn. Remove pin before stitching.

✱ Making half-square triangles: Half-square triangles are squares made up of two triangles from different fabrics sewn together along their longest side to form a square.

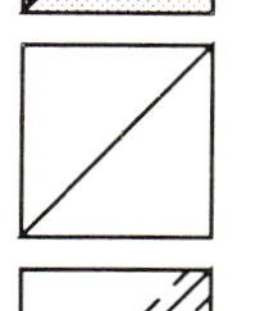

1. Draw a diagonal line on the wrong side of the background fabric square.
2. Pair a background with another fabric square, right sides together. Sew a scant 1/4" seam along either side of the drawn line.

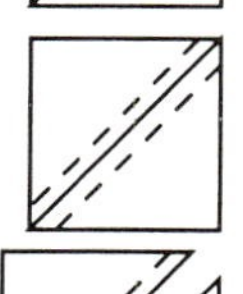

3. Cut on drawn line. Press seams, having lighter fabric pressed toward darker. "Proof" your square to the desired size.

NOTE: to proof square, use a template square that has 1/8" increments and 45° angle marked on it. Line up the angle with the seam, then trim.

✱ Making double half-square triangles: This method is very simple because it doesn't involve cutting any triangles - only squares and rectangles. For purposes of these directions, no specific sizes will be used.

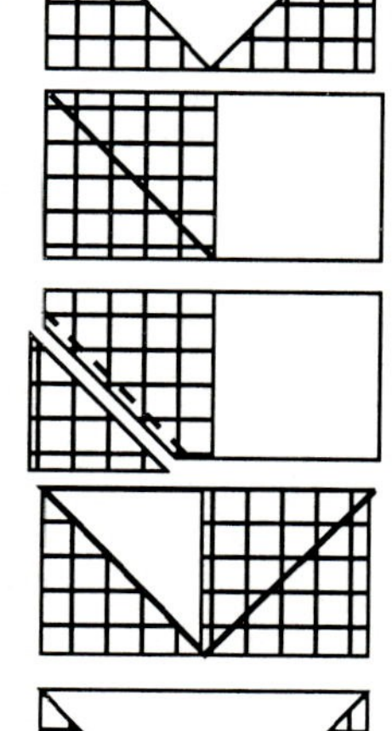

1. With right sides together, line up a square on top of the rectangular piece.
2. Draw a diagonal line through square. Stitch on this line.
3. Trim the excess fabric to within 1/4" of the stitching line.
4. Fold the resulting triangle over the stitching line and press. Take another square and place it on top of this unit. Then repeat steps 1 and 2.
5. Trim off excess fabric once again. Fold over resulting triangle and press.

✱ Making quarter-square triangles: When using this technique, pay attention to fabric pairing when using more than two different fabrics. For purposes of these instructions no specific sizes will be used.

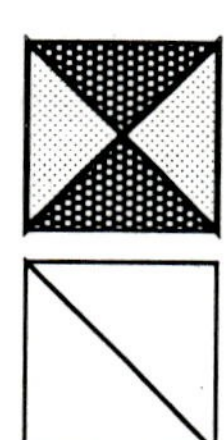

1. Pair up fabrics according to quilt block diagram. Draw a diagonal line on the wrong side of one of the fabrics in each pair.
2. Place fabric pairs right sides together. Stitch a scant 1/4" seam on either side of the drawn line.

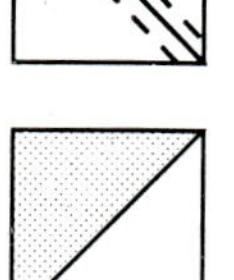

3. Cut on drawn line. Press blocks open, light to dark. Decide now how to pair up the blocks according to quilt block diagram.

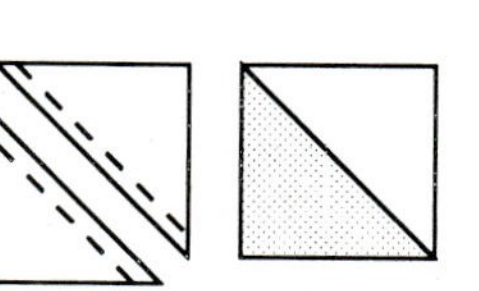

4. Draw a diagonal line on wrong side of one block from each pair. Place blocks right sides together, making sure the seams butt up against one another. Pin, then stitch a scant 1/4" seam on either side of the drawn line.

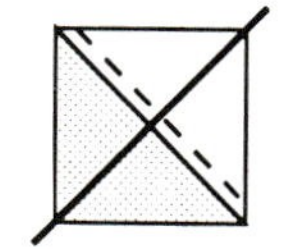

Cut on drawn line. Open and press. 'Proof' your block using a template square that has a 45° angle on it so you don't trim away seam allowances. Line up your seams with the 45° angle for accurate cutting.

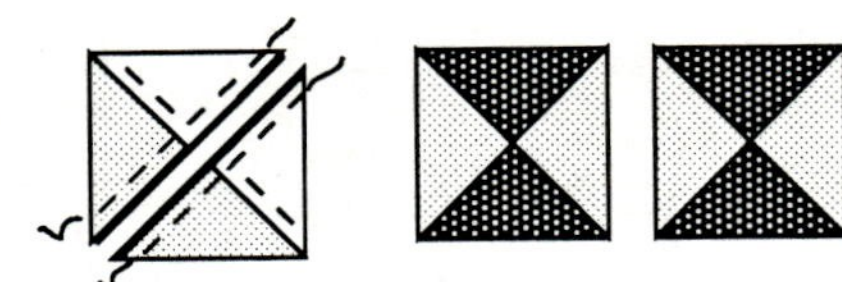

✻ Diagonal sub-cutting: When sub-cutting diagonally, only layer two squares up at a time. Place the template ruler on the diagonal corners, hold firmly, and begin cutting from outer edge to center of the square. Stop cutting at the center. Now finish the cut starting at the opposite corner and meeting at the center cut. By cutting in this manner, there will be no stretching of the square.

✻ Proofing your sewn work: To proof a square, block, rectangle, etc., or whatever you are working on, is to measure it to the size it should be, including the seam allowance. For example: Proof the half-square triangle block to 1-1/2":

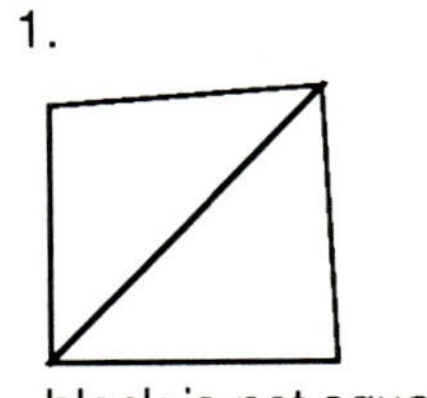

1. Sewn half-square triangle block is not square.
2. Lay a template square which is marked with 1/8" increments and has a 45° angle on it, directly on the block to be proofed. Lay the 45° angle across the seamline.

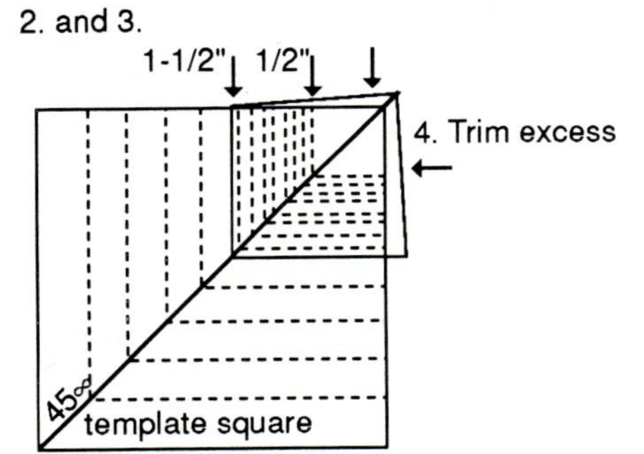

3. Line up the 1-1/2" marks on the ruler as even as possible with your bottom and left block edges.
4. Trim away excess fabric at top and right with the rotary cutter.
5. If necessary, turn the block around to trim the other two sides.

✻ Bordering a quilt: This may be the most overlooked, but important, part of making sure your quilt doesn't "ruffle" around the edges. The quilt ruffles because the borders are too large for the main body of the quilt. Follow these rules for sewing any border to a quilt.

1. Whenever possible, cut border strips from the straight of the fabric rather than the width - there is less stretch.
2. When measuring for a border, measure down the center of the quilt. Cut the two side borders accordingly. Find the center of the border strip and mark it with a pin. Find center of quilt top and mark it with a pin. Now match up pins along with the top and bottom of quilt and border strip. You may have to 'ease' some of the pieced quilt onto the border.
3. Press side borders out. Now measure horizontally through the center of quilt. Cut top and bottom borders according to this measurement. Sew these borders on according to 2. above. Repeat for all borders.

✻ Mitered borders: When borders are seamed at a 45° angle.

1. If there are multiple borders, seam together all strips to form one border strip. Follow same border measurements from above except you must have an excess of border strips which will exceed the actual width and length of the quilt.
2. Center each border on the sides of quilt top. Sew borders on, leaving 1/4" unsewn at the beginning and ending of each seam.
3. Fold quilt in half diagonally, right sides together. Line up the edges of both bottom borders. Lay a triangle even with the folded diagonal edge of quilt and edge of borders. Mark with a pencil the line for the miter onto the border. Refer to diagram for further explanation.

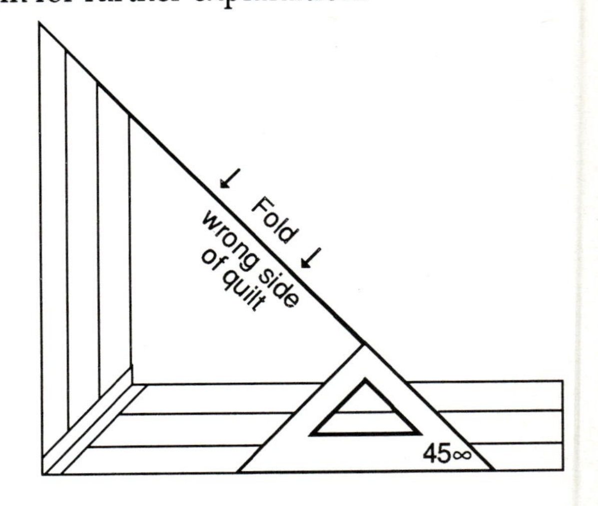

✻ Marking quilting lines: Mark all quilting lines with a water erasable marking pencil. Refer to respective quilt diagrams for quilting lines.

✻ **Machine quilting:** Do not use a hoop or frame. Stitch on lines from center outwards. I use an "invisible" thread on top and bobbin thread to match the quilt backing fabric. Make sure to 'secure' beginning and ending stitches by taking tiny stitches.

✻ **Hand quilting:** Place work in a hoop or frame. Stitch on lines from the center outwards, using a small 'running stitch'.

✻ **Binding:** Trim excess from quilt edges (even up batting and backing). Pin all the way around edge of quilt to hold all layers secure. Cut the required amount of fabric strips to go around quilt. Seam strips together along short ends. Press the long strip in half, wrong sides together. Align the raw edges of binding to raw edges of right side of quilt top. Sew binding on with a 1/4" seam, referring to 'Miter tuck' diagram below for sewing of binding around corners. Turn folded edge of the binding to the back side of quilt and slip-stitch in place.

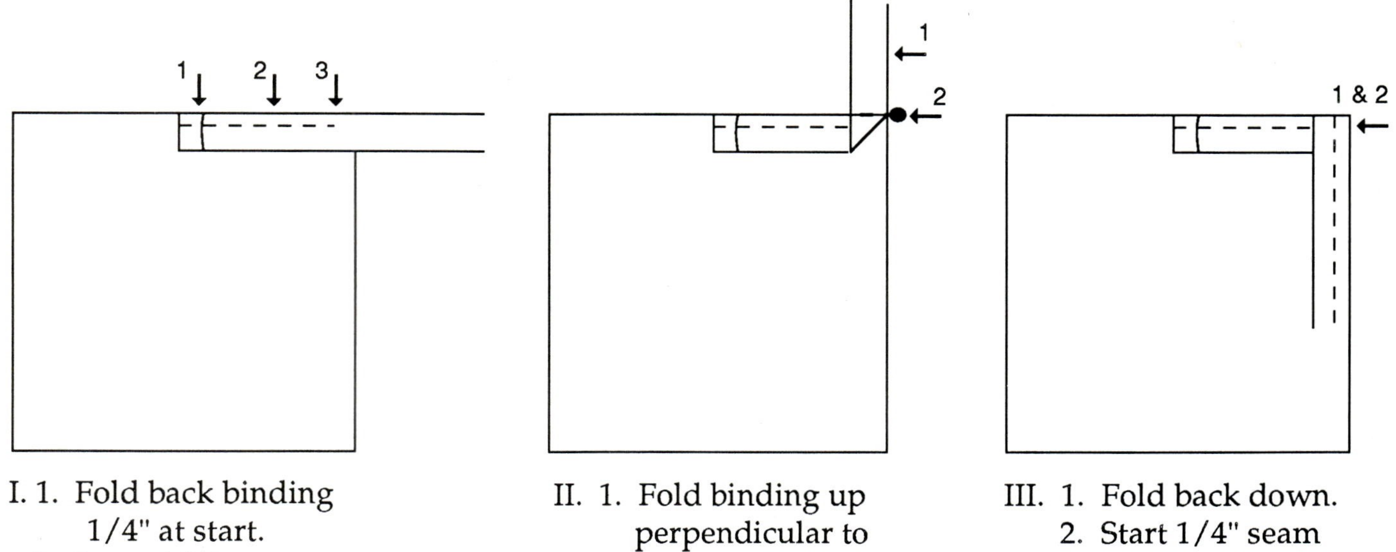

I. 1. Fold back binding 1/4" at start.
2. Seam 1/4".
3. Stop seam 1/4" from quilt edge, back stitch.

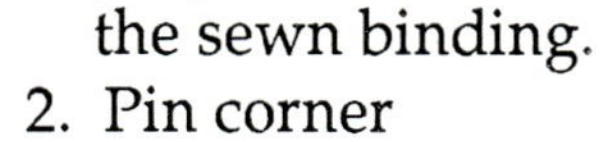

II. 1. Fold binding up perpendicular to the sewn binding.
2. Pin corner

III. 1. Fold back down.
2. Start 1/4" seam at edge of quilt.

Star Placemats

finished size: 14" x 18"

Pre-wash all fabrics. Instructions are for six placemats. Eighteen stars are required.

Fabric requirements:
— 1 yard fabric for placemat fronts (If fabric is not 43" wide, 1-1/4 yards are required)
— 1-1/4 yards batting (Thermolam or Pellon fleece)
— 1-5/8 yards backing fabric (also used for narrow border strips)
— Scrap fabric for the stars in light, medium, and dark values.

Cutting instruction:
For stars:
Note: for *one* star only - unfinished size: 4-1/2" x 4-1/2"
Background:
1. Cut 4 - 1-1/2" x 1-1/2" squares
2. Cut 4 - 1-1/2" x 2-1/2" rectangles
Points:
1. Cut 8 - 1-1/2" squares
Center:
1. Cut 1 - 2-1/2" x 2-1/2" square
Fabric for placemat fronts:
1. Cut 6 pieces 14" x 14"
2. Cut 2 strips 1-1/4" wide. Sub-cut into 12 pieces 1-1/4" x 4-1/2"
Backing and border:
1. Cut 12 strips 3/4" wide
2. Cut 6 pieces 14" x 18"
Batting:
1. Cut 6 pieces 14-1/2" x 18-1/2"

Star block construction: for *one* star
1. Retrieve the 4 pre-cut 1-1/2" x 2-1/2" background rectangles. Retrieve the 8 pre-cut 1-1/2" x 1-1/2" point fabric squares.
2. Draw a diagonal line on the wrong side of the 8 point squares (1-1/2" x 1-1/2").
3. Refer to General Instructions for "Making double half-square triangles". Proof the pieces to be 1-1/2" x 2-1/2". x 4

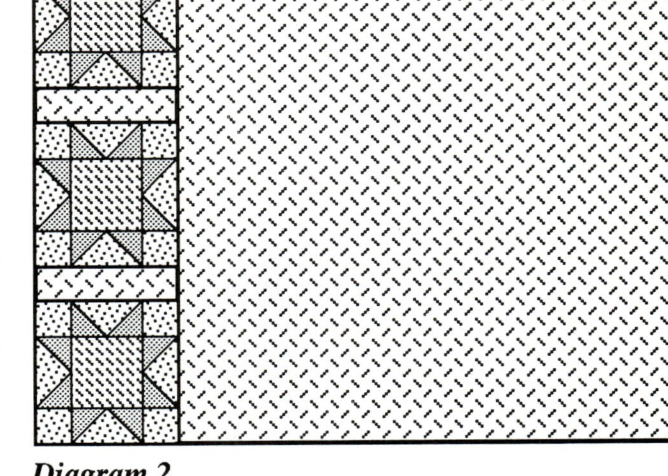

Diagram 2.

4. Follow Diagram 1 to assemble star block. The arrows show the direction for pressing.

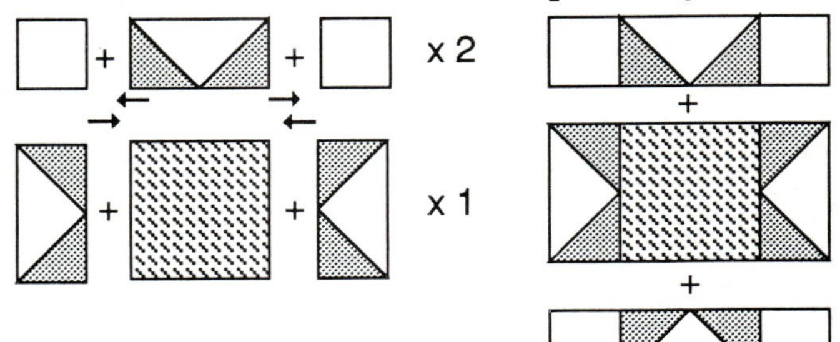

Diagram 1. *Join sections, butting seams. Press. Blocks should measure 4-1/2" x 4-1/2". Make a total of 18 star blocks.*

Placemat assembly: for *one* placemat
1. Choose 3 star blocks for placemat front. Retrieve 2 pre-cut 1-1/4" x 4-1/2" pieces and one fabric front piece.
2. Seam a 1-1/4" x 4-1/2" piece to the bottom of two star blocks. Press. Seam these pieces together to equal a 14" long strip. See Diagram 2. Seam a front piece to this strip, having right sides together. Press. See Diagram 2.
3. Retrieve 2 pre-cut 3/4" wide border strips. Carefully stitch a strip to the top and bottom of the placemat front. Press out. Stitch a border strip to the sides of placemat. Press out.
4. Lay the pre-cut piece of backing fabric, right side up on top of the batting piece. Lay placemat top, right sides together, on these pieces. Pin. Stitch around edges, leaving a 3" opening at the bottom for turning.

5. Turn right sides out. Slip-stitch the opening closed.
6. Machine quilt around the star blocks and the skinny borders stitch-in-a-ditch fashion.
7. Repeat for remaining placemats.

Star coaster

Instructions for *one* coaster: 4-1/2" x 4-1/2"
1. Cut and stitch one star according to directions under Star Placemats.
2. Cut one 3/4" strip of backing, one back 5" x 5", and one batting 5" x 5".

Coaster assembly:
1. Stitch a 3/4" x 4-1/2" piece of border fabric to the top and bottom of star block. Press out.
2. Stitch a 3/4" x 5" piece of border fabric to the right and left sides of star block. Press out.
3. Now refer to #3-7 under Placemat assembly for finishing.

HOT CRANBERRY TODDY

6 cups cranberry juice cocktail
2 cups water
1/2 cup sugar
3 1-in. long strips lemon peel
1/4 cup lemon juice
3 inches stick cinnamon
1 teaspoon whole cloves
Optional: 1/3 cup bourbon or rum

—In a 4 quart saucepan combine cranberry juice cocktail, water, sugar, and lemon juice. Tie lemon peel, cinnamon, and cloves in a 6-inch piece of cheesecloth or muslin. Add spice bag to saucepan. Bring just to boiling; reduce heat. Simmer, covered, 10 minutes. Discard spice bag. Add bourbon or rum.
—Transfer to a heatproof serving carafe or pot. Serve with lemon peel strip and cinnamon stick in each cup. Makes about 10 (7-ounce) servings.

Square Within a Square Placemat

finished size 14"x 18"

Pre-wash all fabrics. Instructions are for six placemats. Eighteen square within a square blocks are required.

Fabric requirements:
— 1 yard fabric for placemat fronts (If fabric is not 43" wide, 1-1/4 yards are required)
— 1-1/4 yards batting (Thermolam or Pellon fleece)
— 1-5/8 yards backing fabric (also used for narrow border strips)
— Scrap fabric for the blocks in light, medium, and dark values.

Cutting instructions:
For square within a square block: *Note: for one block only - unfinished size: 4-1/2" x 4-1/2"
Fabric A: 1 piece 2-1/2" x 2-1/2"
Fabric B: 2 pieces 2-5/16" x 2-5/16" (a little over 2-1/4") Sub-cut in half diagonally once ⧄ =4.
Fabric C: 2 pieces 2-7/8" x 2-7/8". Sub-cut in half diagonally once ⧄ =4.
Fabric for placemat fronts:
— Cut 6 pieces 14" x 14"
— Cut 2 strips 1-1/4" wide. Sub-cut into 12 pieces 1-1/4" x 4-1/2"
Backing and border:
— Cut 12 strips 3/4" wide.
— Cut 6 pieces 14" x 18"
Batting:
— Cut 6 pieces 14-1/2" x 18-1/2"

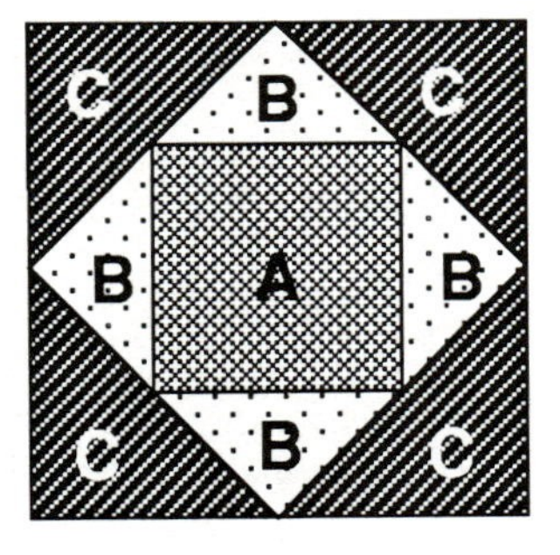

Diagram 1.

Square within a square block assembly: (for one block)
1. Sew 2 triangle fabric pieces B to opposite sides of square A. Press out. Repeat for other two sides. Press out. "Proof" to 3-3/8" square.
2. Sew 2 triangle fabric pieces C to opposite sides of block. Press out. Repeat for other two sides. Press out. "Proof" to 4-1/2" square. Repeat for the other 17 blocks.

Placemat assembly: (for one placemat)
1. Choose 3 blocks for placemat front. Retrieve 2

pre-cut 1-1/4" x 4-1/2" pieces and one fabric front piece.
2. Seam a 1-1/4" x 4-1/2" piece to the bottom of two blocks. Press. Seam these pieces together to equal a 14" long strip. See Diagram 2. Seam a front piece to this strip, having right sides together. Press.
3. Retrieve 2 pre-cut 3/4" wide border strips. Carefully seam a strip to the top and bottom of placemat front. Press out. Stitch a border strip to the sides of placemat. Press out.
4. Lay the pre-cut piece of backing fabric, right side up, on top of the batting piece. Lay placemat top, right sides together, on these pieces. Pin. Stitch around edges, leaving a 3" opening at the bottom for turning.
5. Turn right sides out. Slip-stitch the opening closed.
6. Machine quilt around the blocks and the skinny borders stitch-in-a-ditch fashion.
7. Repeat for remaining placemats.

***Diagram* 2.**

Square Within a Square Coaster

Instruction for one coaster, 4-1/2" x 4-1/2"
1. Cut and stitch one block according to directions under placemat cutting instructions.
2. Cut one 3/4" wide strip of backing, one back 5" x 5", and one batting 5" x 5".

Coaster assembly:
1. Stitch a 3/4" x 4-1/2" piece of border fabric to the top and bottom of block. Press out.
2. Stitch a 3/4" x 5" piece of border fabric to the sides. Press out.
3. Now refer to #3-7 under Placemat assembly for finishing.

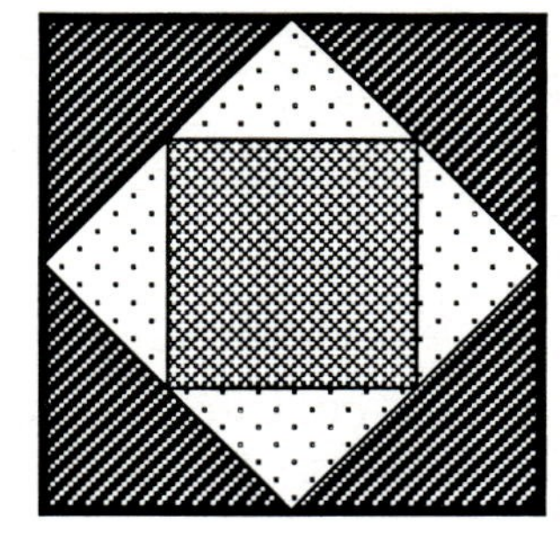

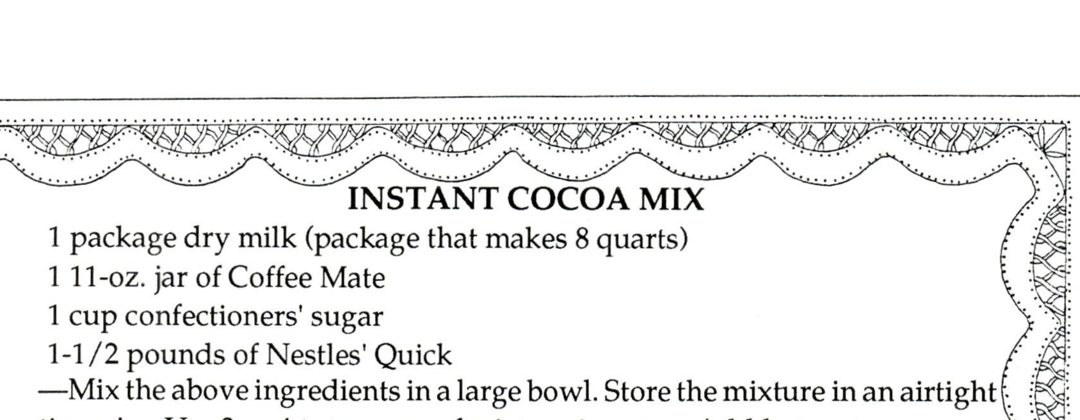

INSTANT COCOA MIX

1 package dry milk (package that makes 8 quarts)
1 11-oz. jar of Coffee Mate
1 cup confectioners' sugar
1-1/2 pounds of Nestles' Quick
—Mix the above ingredients in a large bowl. Store the mixture in an airtight tin or jar. Use 3 or 4 teaspoons of mixture in a cup. Add hot water.

Spice Mat

finished size: 9" x 9"

Pre-wash all fabrics. The spice mat has been designed with a removable spice bag to enable laundering of the mat.

Fabric and supplies requirements:
— 2" strip background fabric
— 2" strip star point fabric
— 1/3 yard border, backing, and star center
— 1/3 yard muslin
— 1/3 yard low loft batting
— 2-3 tablespoons whole cloves or crushed cinnamon sticks (or any other spice)

Cutting instructions:
For star block:
1. Background: Cut 1 strip 2" wide. Sub-cut into 4 squares 2" x 2" and 4 rectangles 2" x 3-1/2".
2. Points: Cut 1 strip 2" wide. Sub-cut into 8 squares 2" x 2".
3. Center: Cut 1 piece 3-1/2" x 3-1/2".
Border strips and backing:
1. Cut 1 strip 2" wide. Sub-cut into 2 strips: 2" x 6-1/2" and 2 strips 2" x 9-1/2".
2. Cut one square 9-1/2" x 9-1/2".
Muslin and batting:
1. Cut 2 pieces batting 9-1/2" x 9-1/2". Cut 2 pieces batting 6" x 6".
2. Cut 2 pieces muslin 9-1/2" x 9-1/2". Cut 2 pieces muslin 6" x 6".

Star block construction:
1. Retrieve the 4 background 2" x 3-1/2" pieces and the 8 point squares 2" x 2".
2. Draw a diagonal line on the wrong side of all point pieces. Now refer to "Making double half-square triangles" in the General Instructions. Proof these to 2" x 3-1/2".

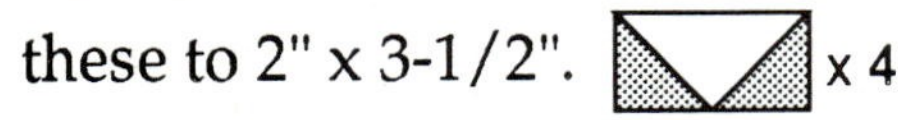

3. Follow Diagram 1 to assemble star block. The arrows show direction for pressing.
4. Seam 2 pre-cut 2" x 6-1/2" strips of border to right and left sides of block. Press out. Seam the remaining 2 pre-cut 2" x 9-1/2" strips to top and bottom. Press out. Mat top should be 9-1/2" x 9-1/2".

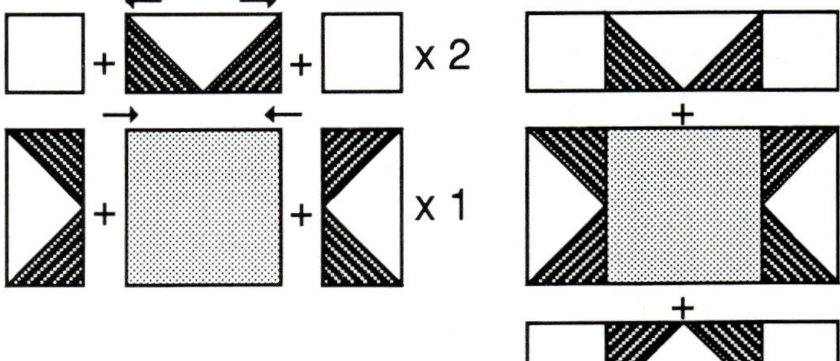

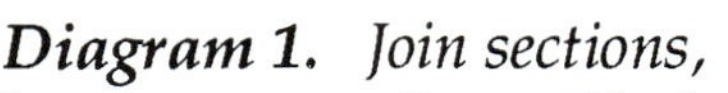

Diagram 1. *Join sections, butting seams. Press. Block should measure 6-1/2" x 6-1/2".*

Mat construction:

1. Machine baste a piece of pre-cut batting to the wrong side of the block square using a 1/8" seam allowance. Baste remaining piece of batting to wrong side of backing square.
2. Lay the squares from step #1 right sides together and seam 1/4" around the three sides. Backstitch. Turn right sides out. Press lightly at seam edges.
3. Place the pre-cut muslin squares right sides together and seam around (1/4") the three sides, leaving the top open and a 3" space open at the bottom. See Diagram 2.
4. Slip the star block section into the sewn muslin pocket, having right sides together. Line up and pin the raw edges at the top edge. Seam around the top edges, matching the side seams. Do not stitch a flat seam so as to close the top. See Diagram 3 for stitching.
5. Turn the pieces right side out through the hole in the muslin lining. Slip stitch the muslin edge closed. Tuck muslin pocket into star pocket.
6. Stitch-in-a-ditch *through all thicknesses*, around the star block on *three* sides. Leave the "top" side unstitched (the one parallel to the opening).

open

Muslin

open

Diagram 2.

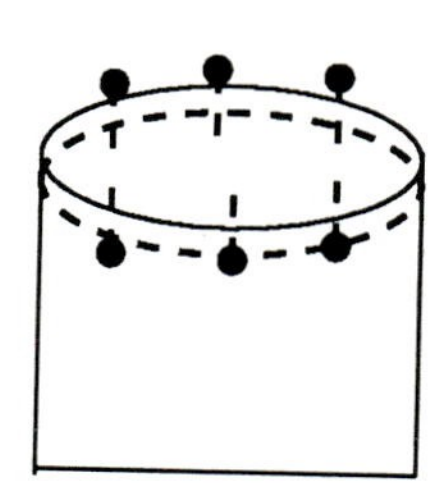

Diagram 3.

Spice packet:

1. Baste pre-cut muslin 6" squares to batting.
2. Place right sides together and seam, leaving a 3" opening. Place cloves or crushed cinnamon sticks in spice bag. Seam opening closed. Insert spice bag into pocket of mat.

CHERRY JAM

Makes 6 cups

3 pounds sour cherries
5 cups sugar
1 box fruit pectin

—Wash jar lids, jars, and bands. Sterilize jars for 10 minutes. Remove stems and pits from 3 pounds of sour cherries. Finely chop cherries, 1/4 inch pieces. Measure 4 cups chopped cherries into large pot. Measure 5 cups sugar into a bowl. Drain jars. Add 1 box of fruit pectin to fruit. Bring to full rolling boil over high heat, stirring constantly. Quickly add sugar to fruit. Bring to full rolling boil, stirring constantly, then, continue boiling for 1 minute, stirring constantly. Remove from heat. Skim off any foam with a metal spoon. Fill jars immediately to 1/8" of tops. Wipe jar rims and threads. Cover quickly with lids. Screw bands tightly.

Bow Placemats

finished size: 17-1/2" x 21-1/2"

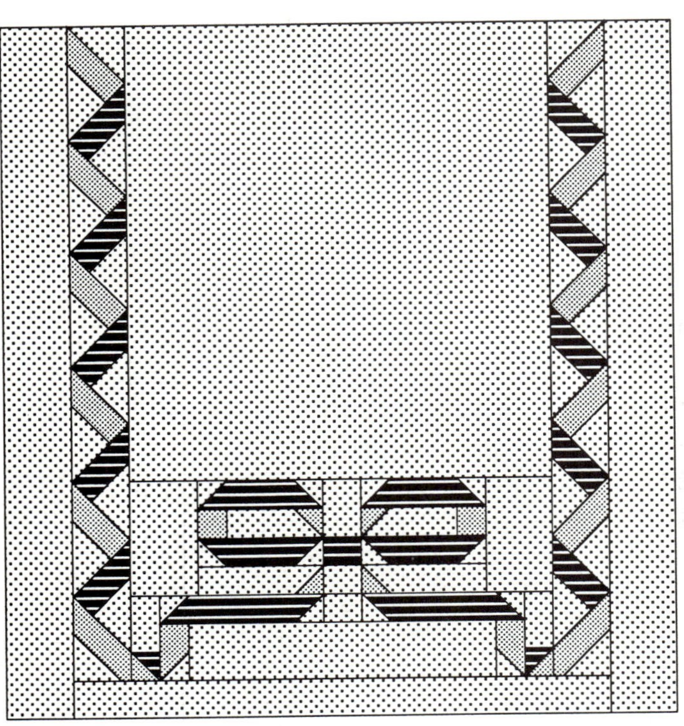

Instructions are for 6 placemats, 17-1/2" x 21-1/2" (The bow placemat is designed to have the bow hang over the edge of the table.) Pre-wash all fabric and flannel.

Fabric requirements:
—2-1/4 yards background fabric (a non-directional fabric works best)
—1/2 yard dark fabric
—1/2 yard medium fabric
—2 yards backing fabric
—2 yards cotton flannel (used instead of batting)

Cutting for bows only:
*NOTE: It is very beneficial to mark your cut pieces with the corresponding letters as you cut.

Background:

1. Cut 1 strip 3-1/2" wide. Sub-cut into 12 - 2-1/4" x 3-1/2" pieces A (for one placemat: 2)
   Sub-cut 12 - 1-1/4" x 3-1/2" pieces B (for one placemat: 2)
2. Cut 2 strips 2" wide. Sub-cut into 6 - 2" x 8" pieces G (for one placemat: 1).
   Sub-cut 6 - 1-1/2" x 2" pieces H (for one placemat: 1)
3. Cut 5 strips 1-1/4" wide. Sub-cut into 84 - 1-1/4" x 1-1/4" pieces C (for one placemat: 14).
   Sub-cut 12 - 1-1/4" x 2-3/4" pieces D (for one placemat: 2).
   Sub-cut 12 - 1-1/4" x 1-1/2" pieces E (for one placemat: 2).
   Sub-cut 12 - 1-1/4" x 2" pieces J (for one placemat: 2).

Dark:

1. Cut 4 strips 1-1/4" wide. Sub-cut into 24 - 1-1/4" x 3-1/2" pieces B (for one placemat: 4).
   Sub-cut into 6 - 1-1/4 x 1-1/2" pieces E (for one placemat: 1).
   Sub-cut into 12 - 1-1/4" x 4-1/2" pieces F (for one placemat: 2).
2. Cut 1 strip 1-5/8" wide. Sub-cut 6 - 1-5/8" x 1-5/8" pieces K (for one placemat: 1).

Medium:

1. Cut 2 strips 1-1/4" wide. Sub-cut into 36 - 1-1/4" x 1-1'4" pieces C (for one placemat: 6).
   Sub-cut into 12 - 1-1/4" x 2" pieces I (for one placemat: 2).
2. Cut 1 strip 1-5/8" wide. Sub-cut into 6 - 1-5/8" x 1-5/8" pieces K (for one placemat: 1).

Construction for one bow:

1. To assemble 4 units CBC: C B C x 4 Retrieve 4 dark pieces B and 8 background pieces C.
2. Draw a diagonal line on the wrong side of all background pieces C ◸ .
3. Place the background pieces right sides together on pieces B according to Diagram 1. Sew, just inside the drawn line nearest to the corner.
4. Press the corner out. Trim away only the dark triangle of fabric. Set aside.
5. To assemble 2 units of CDC: Retrieve the 2 pre-cut background pieces D and the 4 medium pieces C.
6. Draw a diagonal line on the wrong side of 2 of the 4 medium pieces C. Place these pieces on the background D pieces, right sides together. See Diagram 2. *NOTE: the units are mirror images.
7. Press the corner and the seam towards center of unit. Trim away only the light triangle of fabric. Stitch a C medium square to these units referring to Diagram 2.
8. To assemble units BC: Retrieve 2 background pieces B and 2 medium pieces C. Draw a diagonal line on the wrong side of the C pieces. Place them right sides together on the B pieces according to Diagram 3. Once again these units are mirror images. Stitch just inside the line. Press out. Trim. See Diagram 3.
9. Retrieve background pieces H and E. Retrieve dark piece E. Stitch this unit together according to Diagram 4. Press dark to light.
10. Pin and stitch units together as shown in Diagram 5.
11. Stitch a background A piece to the right and left sides of bow. See Diagram 5.
12. Retrieve 2 dark pieces F and 4 background C's. Draw a diagonal line on the wrong side of the C's. Place C's right sides together on F pieces, keeping in mind these pieces are also mirror images. See Diagram 6. Add piece E according to Diagram 6.
13. Retrieve 2 medium I's and 2 background C's. Draw a diagonal line on the wrong side of C's. Place on I according to diagram. These are mirror images. Stitch and trim as previously done. See Diagram 7.

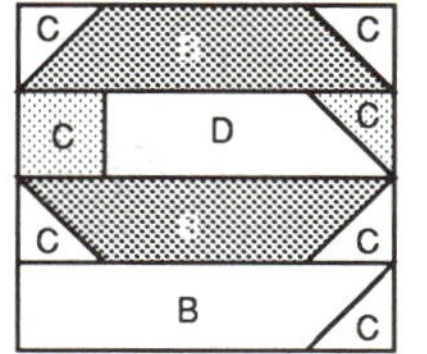

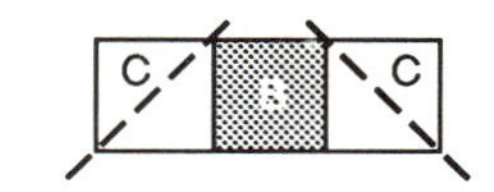

Diagram 1.

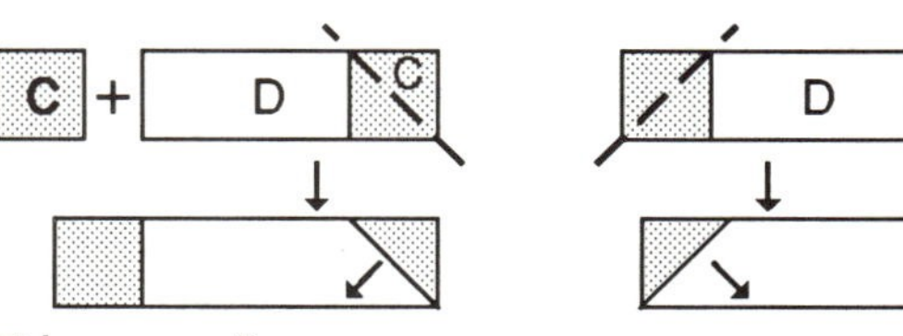

Diagram 2.

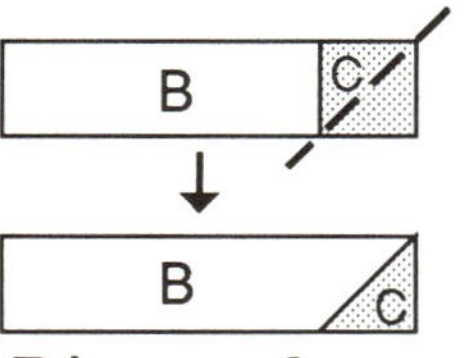

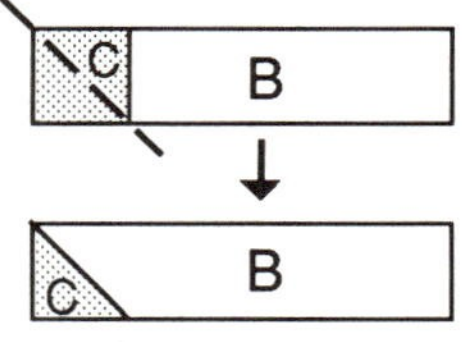

Diagram 3.

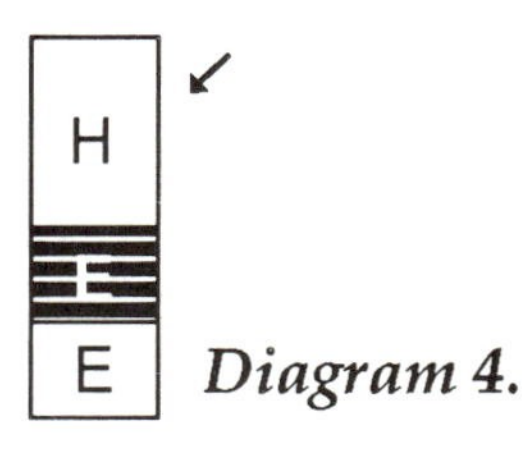

Diagram 4.

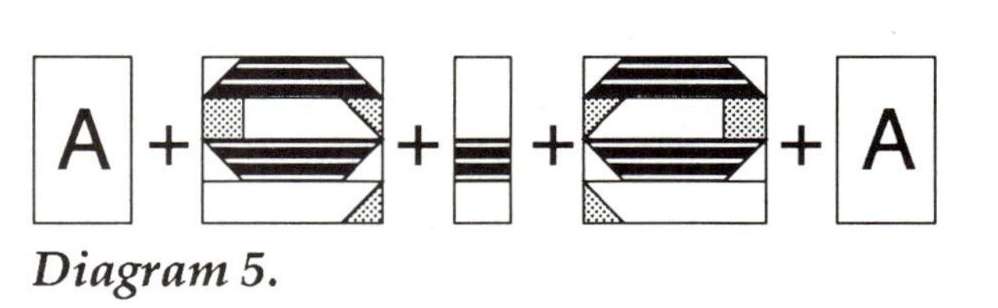

Diagram 5.

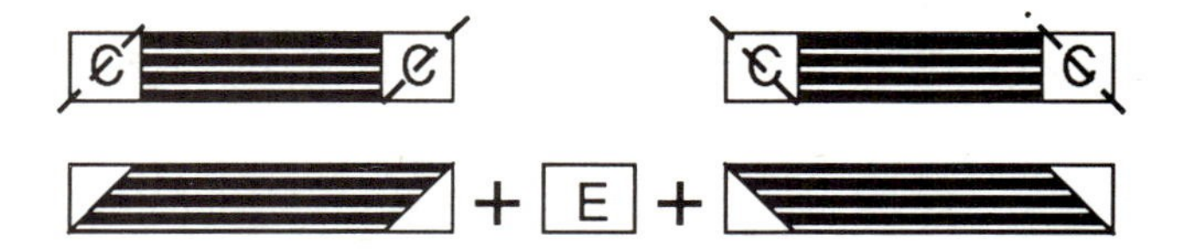

Diagram 6. Stitch just inside drawn line, press out, trim out dark triangle. Stitch background Piece E to completed units. Seam these units to background piece G.

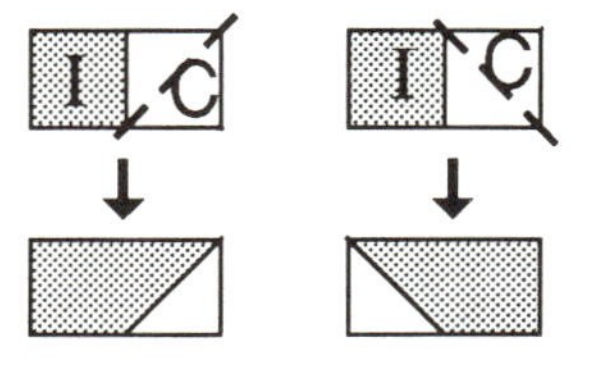

Diagram 7.

14. Add unit from Step #13 (Diagram 7) to unit just completed. See Diagram 8.

15. Retrieve a dark K and a medium K. Draw a diagonal line on the wrong side of the medium K. Proceed to General Instructions for "Making half-square triangles". "Proof" (see General Instructions) to 1-1/4" x 1-1/4".

16. Retrieve 2 background pieces J. Stitch them to the K units just made in Step #15. The units are reverse images. See Diagram 9.

17. Pin and stitch the units together as illustrated in Diagram 10. The bow block should measure 5-3/4" x 11".

18. Pin and stitch completed units from #17 and #10. See Diagram 11.

Cutting for pieced borders and borders:

Background: for all six placemats.

1. Cut 3 strips 3-1/4" wide. Sub-cut into 33 - 3-1/4" x 3-1/4" squares. Sub-cut again diagonally twice to yield 132 triangles L. (for one placemat: 22).

2. Cut 1 strip 2-1/8" wide. Sub-cut into 6 - 2-1/8" x 2-1/8". Sub-cut in half diagonally once to yield 12 triangles M (for one placemat: 2).

3. Cut 2 strips 2" wide. Sub-cut into 6 - 2" x 3" pieces N, and 6 - 2" x 5" pieces O. With right side of fabric facing up, make a 45° angle cut along the left side of pieces N and O. See Diagram 12.

4. Cut 2 strips 1-1/2" wide. Sub-cut into 6 - 14" long strips. These strips will be sewn to the bottom of the placemat later.

5. Cut 2 strips 15-1/2" wide. Sub-cut into 6 pieces 11" x 15-1/2". These are the placemat centers.

6. Cut 6 strips 2-1/4" wide. Sub-cut into 12 pieces 2-1/4" x 21". (side length).

Dark fabric: for all six placemats

1. Cut 6 strips a "hair" under 1-1/4" wide.

Medium fabric: for all six placemats

1. Cut 6 strips a "hair" under 1-1/4" wide.

Backing and lining: for all six placemats

1. Cut 6 pieces 17-1/2" x 21-1/2" from the backing fabric and the flannel. (You may want to make sure of the exact size of *your* placemat first!)

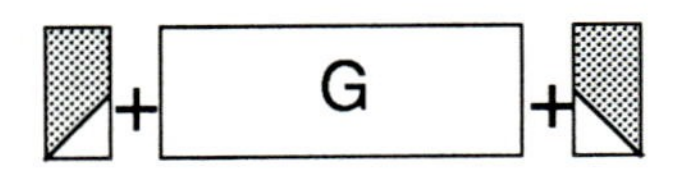

Diagram 8.

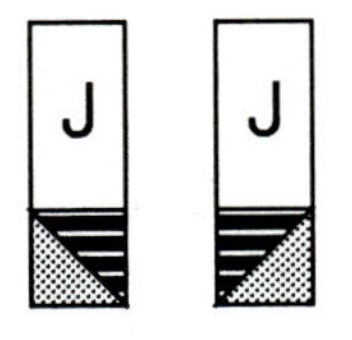

Diagram 9.

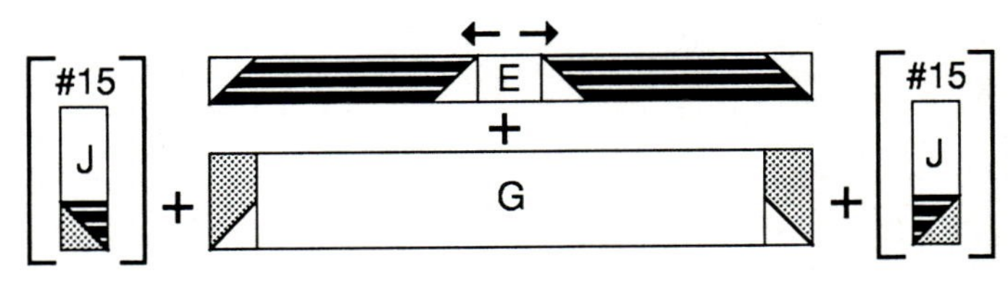

Diagram 10.

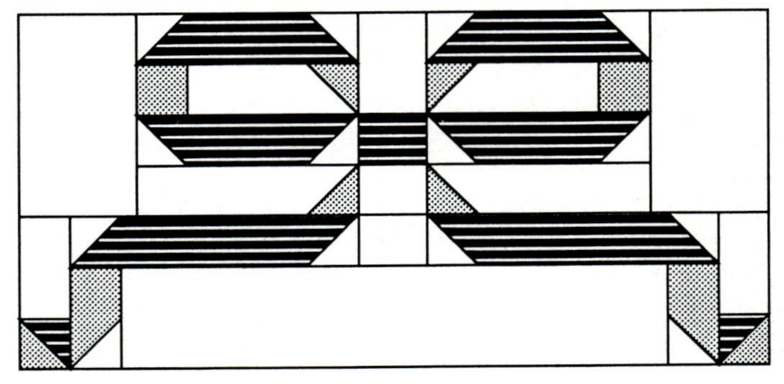

Diagram 11.

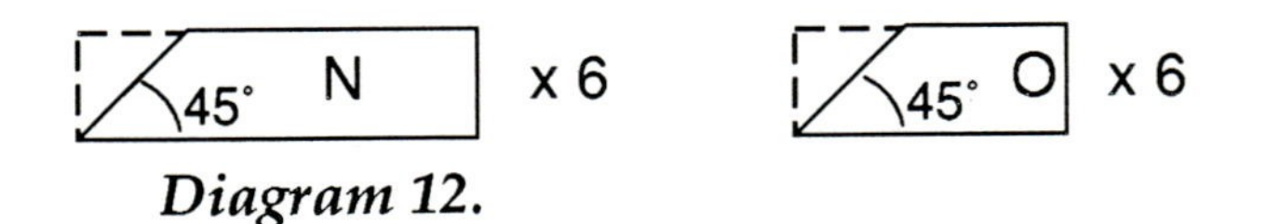

Diagram 12.

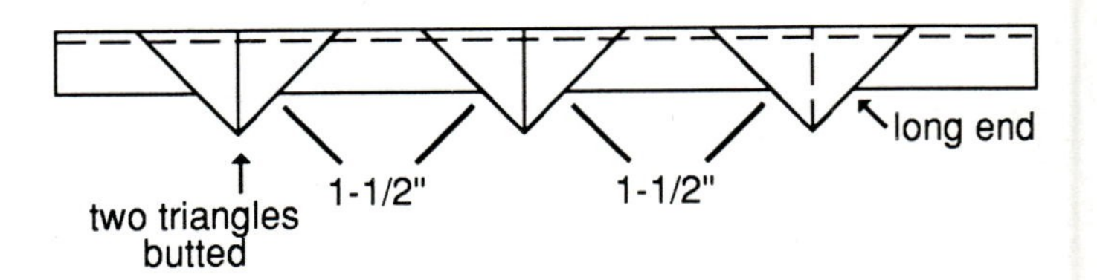

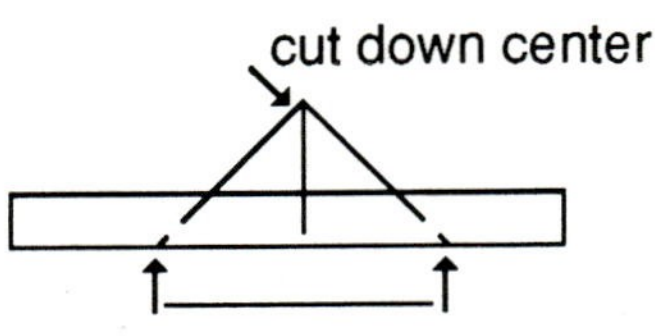

Diagram 13.

*Press triangles towards strip.

*Lay template ruler on triangles and trim

Stitching the pieced border: (borders for one placemat)

1. Retrieve 22 triangles L, 1 strip 1-1/4" wide of medium, and 1 strip 1-1/4" wide of dark.
2. Stitch 12 triangles to the dark strip and 10 triangles to the medium strip according to Diagram 13. Remember to allow an 1-1/2" margin between the pairs of triangles and at the beginning of strip.
3. Retrieve 2 background triangles M, for corners. Stitch these corners onto the remaining medium strip from step #2 along the triangles *long* side. See Diagram 14. Remember to leave an 1-1/2" margin between the triangles. Press and cut as in Diagram 13.
4. Assemble the right and left borders according to Diagram 15. (will have 1 dark triangle left over). Press after each triangle piece is added. Add the corner pieces last. **NOTE: the bottom corner pieces extend beyond the border edge. Trim the corner so it is even with the border strip.

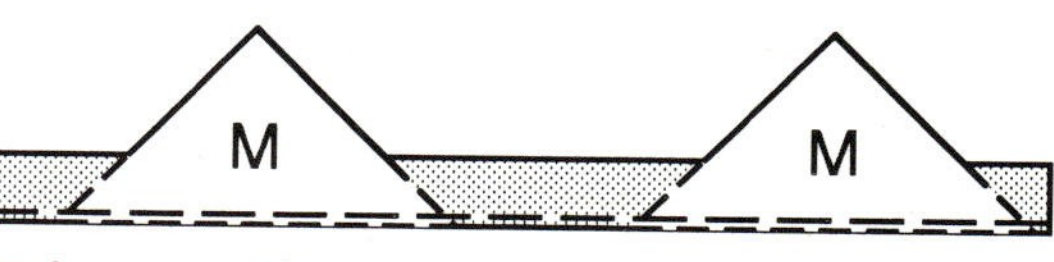

Diagram 14.

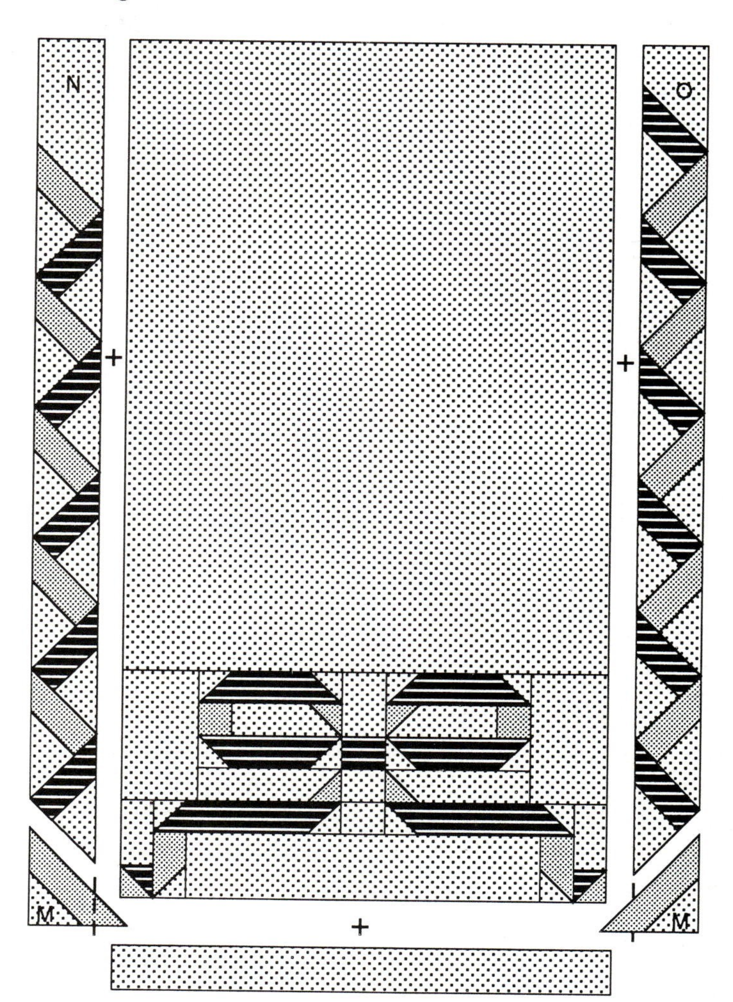

Diagram 15.

Placemat assembly: for one placemat

1. Pin and stitch the 11" x 15-1/2" pre-cut piece of background fabric to the top of the bow block. Press.
2. Pin and stitch the pieced borders to the right and left sides of placemat. (The top edges of the border will extend beyond the center piece. Simply trim away the excess.) See Diagram 15.
3. Stitch a pre-cut 1-1/2" x 14" strip of background to the bottom of placemat. Press.
4. Stitch the pre-cut 2-1/4" wide side strips to the right and left sides of placemat. Press. Refer to Diagram 15.
5. Retrieve the pre-cut 17-1/2" x 21-1/2" pieces of backing and flannel. If you have not cut them yet, check the size of your placemat and cut them out now. One piece of flannel and one backing piece is needed for each placemat.
6. Smooth out the flannel piece on a flat surface. Place the backing fabric, right side up, on top of flannel. Next, place the placemat, right sides together, on top of the backing fabric. Pin and stitch through all layers (1/4" seam). Leave a 3"-4" opening in one of the sides for turning.
7. Turn right side out and press. Slip-stitch opening closed. Top-stitch 1/8"-1/4" in from the edge of placemat.

Bow Napkin Holders

Fabric and supply requirements:
— 3/8 yard fabric
— small amount of polyester fiberfil

Cutting instructions:
1. Cut 2 strips 4" wide. Sub-cut into 6 pieces 4" x 9" for bows.
2. Cut 1 strip 1-1/4" wide. Cut this strip in half and put the other half aside.
3. Cut 1 strip 3" wide. Sub-cut into 6 pieces 3" x 7".

Construction:
1. Retrieve a piece 4" x 9". Fold in half along the length of the piece, having right sides together. Diagram 1.
2. Stitch 1-1/2" down from either ends of the piece. See Diagram 2.
3. Refold the piece, still having right sides together, so the seam is now down the center of the piece. See Diagram 3.
4. Stitch the top and bottom seams. See Diagram 4.
5. Turn right side out and stuff lightly.
6. Retrieve the 1-1/4" x 22" strip. Fold in half along the long edge, right sides together, and stitch one short end and the entire length of the strip. Turn right side out and press. Cut this tube into 6 - 3-1/2" long pieces. Place one of these pieces around the bow section, lightly gathering the front. (The turning hole will be turned to the back side.) Overlap and slip stitch the back ends of the tie.
7. Retrieve a 3" x 7" piece for the loop on the napkin holder. Fold the strip right sides together along the long edge. Stitch one short edge and the long edge. Turn right side out. Turn raw edges on the other short end in. Press. Slip stitch the ends together, slightly overlapping. Slip stitch to bow.

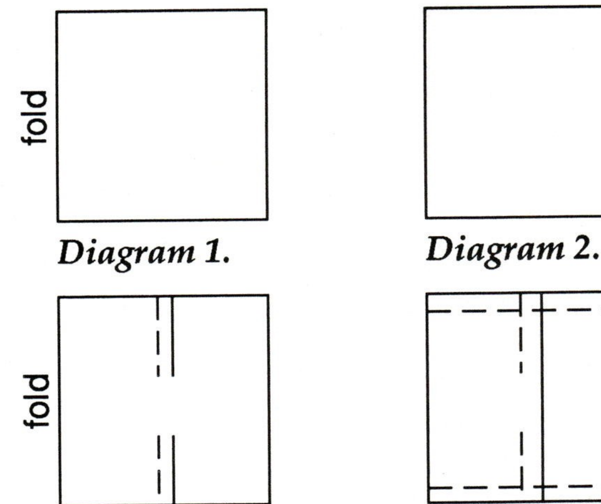

Diagram 1. *Diagram 2.* *Diagram 3.* *Diagram 4.*

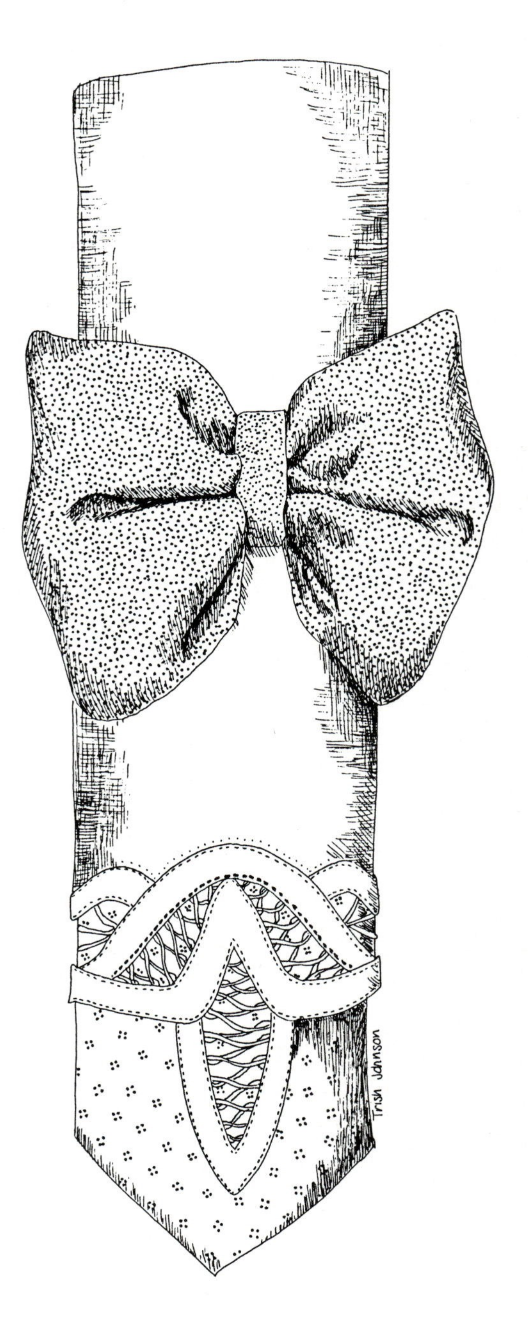

Judy's Table Runner

finished size: 14-1/2" x 44-1/2"

Pre-wash all fabrics. This pattern has been written for the quick-cutting and piecing techniques. Please use a rotary cutter and plastic template ruler.

***Note: Mark all pieces with corresponding letters as you cut.**

Fabric requirements:

— 1/4 yd. light
— 1/3 yd. med. 1 (also used for wide border)
— 1/2 yd. med. 2
— 1 yd. dark (also used for "skinny" border and backing)
— 18" x 48" batting

From light fabric cut:

1. Cut 1 strip 3-1/2" wide. From this strip cut 2 squares 3-1/2" x 3-1/2" for pieces A1.
2. Trim strip down to 3-3/8" wide. Cut 8 pieces 3-3/8" x 3-3/8". Sub-cut in half diagonally in half once, to yield 16 pieces B.
3. Cut 1 strip 3" wide. From this strip cut 12 pieces 3" x 3" for pieces C.

Medium 1:

1. Cut 4 pieces 4" x 4" for pieces I
2. Cut 3 strips 3" wide for borders

Medium 2:

1. Cut 1 strip 3-1/2" wide. From this strip cut:
— 2 pieces 3-1/2" x 3-1/2" for pieces A2
2. Trim the leftover strip to 3" wide. Cut 6 pieces 3" x 5-1/2" for pieces D.
3. Cut 1 strip 1-3/4" wide. From this strip cut:
— 20 pieces 1-3/4" x 1-3/4" for pieces E
4. Cut 2 strips 3" wide. From this strip cut:
— 30 pieces 1-3/4" x 3" for pieces F.
4. Cut 1 strip 2-1/4" wide. From this strip cut:
— 19 pieces 2-1/4" x 2-1/4" for pieces G.

Dark:

1. Cut 1 strip 2-1/4" wide. From this strip cut:
— 16 pieces 2-1/4" x 2-1/4" pieces G.
2. Cut 1 strip 2-1/8" wide. From this strip cut:
— 6 pieces 2-1/8" x 2-1/8". Sub-cut once diagonally for pieces H.
3. Cut 2 strips 1-3/4" wide. From this strip cut: 20 pieces 1-3/4" x 1-3/4" for pieces E2.

4. Cut 3 strips 3/4" wide for skinny border. (The same fabric as used for backing.)

Assembling the units:

#I - Making A1A2 half-square triangles :

1. Retrieve 2 light A squares (3-1/2") and 2 medium 2 squares (3-1/2").
2. Draw a diagonal line on the wrong side of the light squares. Now refer to the General Instructions for "Making half-square triangles". Follow instructions, "proof" (see General Instructions for proofing) to be 3" square A1A2. Set aside. Yield - 4.

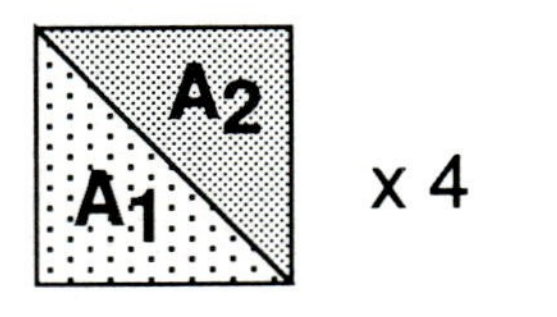

#II - Making double half-square triangles E2FE2:

1. Retrieve 20 dark pieces (1-3/4" square) E2. Draw a diagonal line on the wrong side of all pieces .
2. Retrieve 10 medium 2 pieces F (1-3/4" x 3"). Proceed to General Instructions for "Making double half-square triangles". Yield 10.

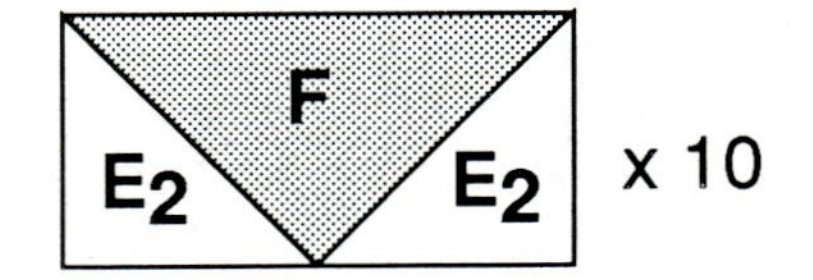

#III - "Making double half-square triangles CDC:

1. Retrieve 6 pieces D (3" x 5-1/2") and 12 pieces C (3" x 3").
2. Draw a diagonal line on the wrong side of all pieces C. Refer to "Making double half-square triangles" in the General Instructions. Yield - 6.

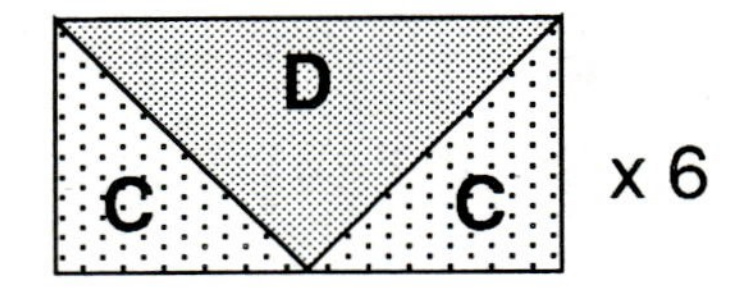

#IV - Making units I4B :

1. Retrieve 16 light pieces B and 4 pieces Medium 1. Stitch a triangle to the right and left sides of I. Press out. Stitch 2 triangles to the top and bottom. Press out. "Proof" unit to be 5-1/2" x 5-1/2". Yield - 4.

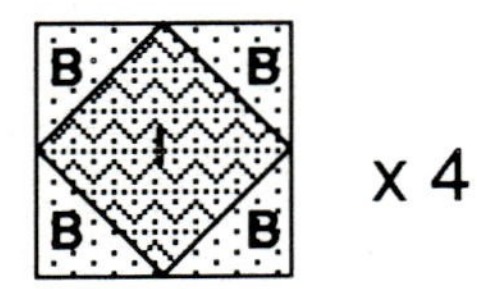

#V - "Making half-square triangles" G1G2 :

1. Retrieve 16 medium 2 pieces G1 (2-1/4" x 2-1/4") and 16 dark pieces G2 (2-1/4" square).
2. Draw a diagonal line on the wrong side of all the light pieces. Refer to "Making half-square triangles" in the General Instructions. "Proof" to 1-3/4" x 1-3/4". Yield - 32.

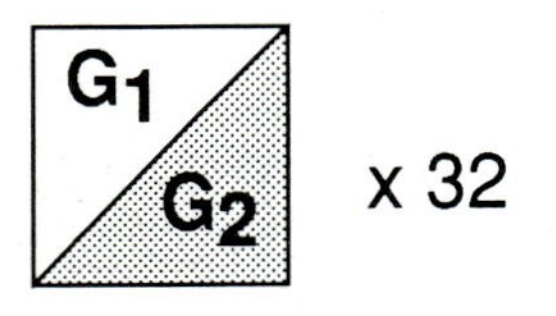

#VI - Making units G4H

1. Retrieve 3 pieces G (2-1/4" square) of medium 2 fabric and 12 dark pieces H.
2. Repeat the same steps as in IV. Proof to 3" x 3". Yield - 3.

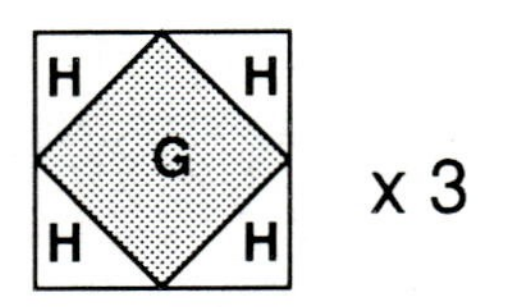

Stitching units together:

1. Piece 10 units together according to Diagram 1. Arrows show direction for pressing.
2. Piece 3 units together according to Diagram 2.
3. Piece 3 units together according to Diagram 3.
4. Piece 4 units together according to Diagram 4.
5. Piece 2 units together according to Diagram 5.
6. Pin and stitch all units together referring to "Whole quilt" diagram.
7. Stitch top and bottom wide borders onto quilt according to "Bordering a quilt" in the General Instructions. Press. Pin and stitch left and right borders on to quilt.
8. Cut 2 - 6" pieces off one of the skinny strips. Seam one 6" piece to each of the other pre-cut strips. Pin and stitch top and bottom skinny borders onto quilt. Press out. Use the remaining strip for the right and left borders. Pin and stitch. Press out.
9. The backing fabric must be pieced. Cut 2 pieces the width of the table runner, by 1/2 the length plus 1/2". Seam and press.
10. Smooth out the batting on a flat surface. Lay the backing piece on top of the batting, right side up. Now lay the table runner on top of that, right sides together. Smooth out. Pin at the edges, through all layers, all the way around the runner.
12. Seam a 1/4" seam all the way around the table runner, leaving 3"-4" on one side open for turning. Turn right side out. Slip-stitch opening closed. Lightly press (cool iron!) along the edge of the table runner. The "skinny" border gives the illusion of a binding.
13. Smooth out the table runner and pin (safety pins) in the center of each square to stabilize. Stitch-in-a-ditch, around the skinny border and inside the wide border. Also stitch-in-a-ditch around individual blocks using invisible thread and bobbin thread to match the backing. (See "Machine quilting" in the General Instructions.)

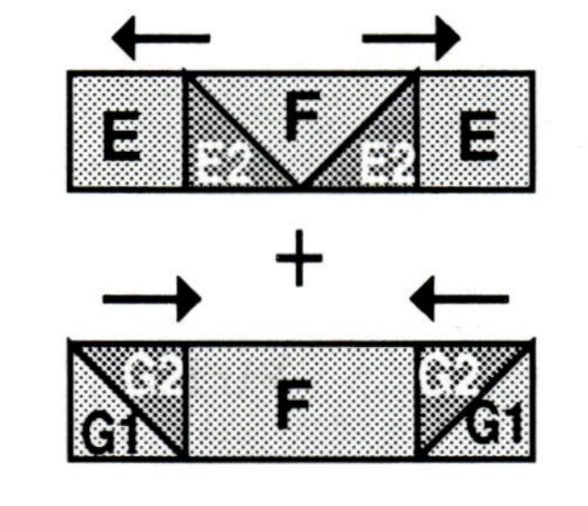

Diagram 1.

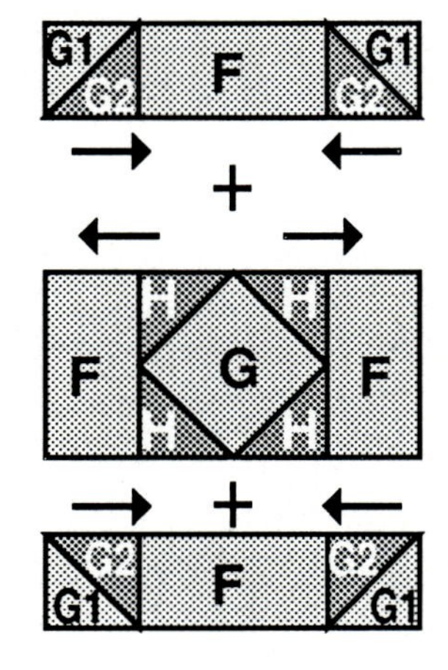

Diagram 2.

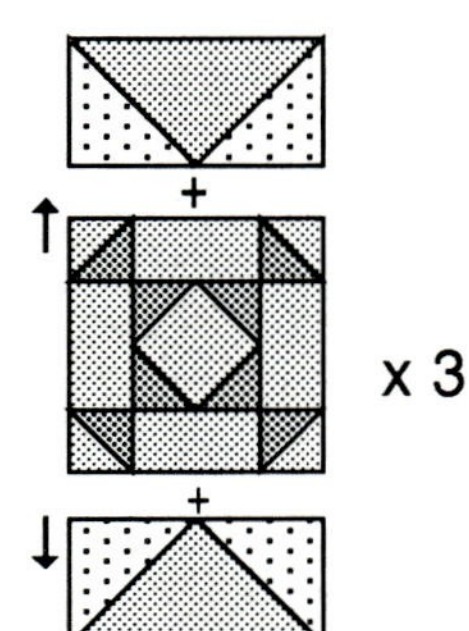

Diagram 3.

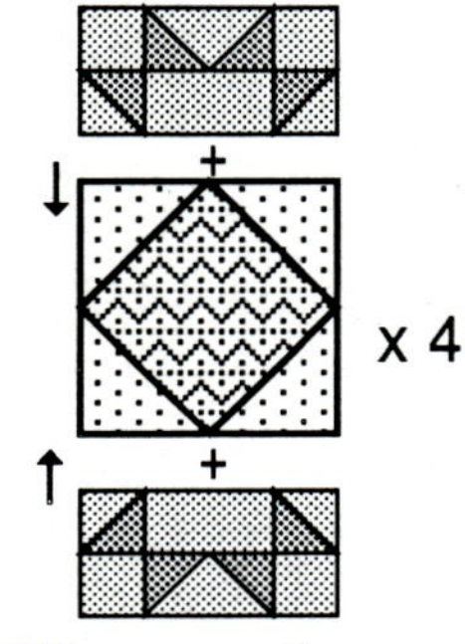

Diagram 4.

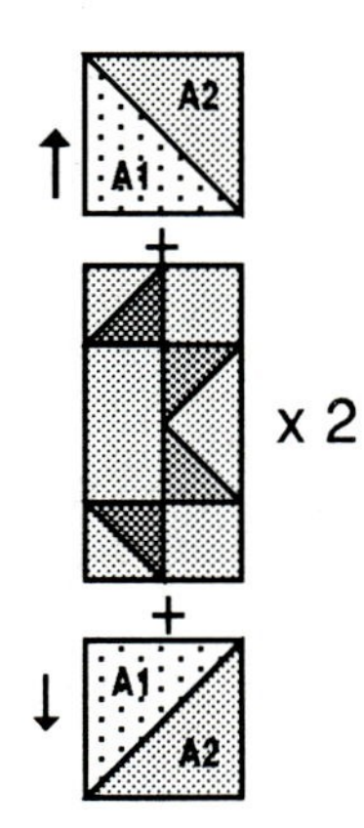

Diagram 5.

Mini Medallion Quilt

finished size: 17" x 21"

Fabric requirements:
— Scraps of light, medium and dark value fabric
— 1/8 yd. 1st border
— 3/4 yd. 2nd (outer border) (1/4 yd. if not striped)
— 5/8 yd. batting
— 5/8 yd. backing
— 1/4 yd. binding

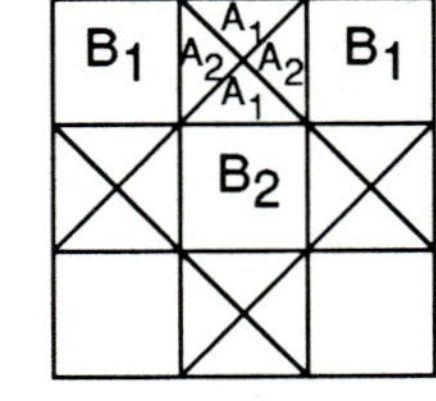

Diagram 1.

Mini Medallion Whole Quilt Diagram.

Step 1:
Center star: unfinished size 3-1/2" square
1. From background cut: 2 pieces A1, (2-1/4" x 2-1/4") and 4 pieces B1, (1-1/2" x 1-1/2")
2. From star point (dark) fabric cut: 2 pieces A2, (2-1/4" x 2-1/4")
3. From "center" fabric cut: 1 piece B2 (1-1/2" x 1-1/2")
Construction of center star:
1. Retrieve 2 background pieces A1 and 2 "point" pieces A2.
2. Draw a diagonal line on the wrong side of the 2 background squares. [⧄] Pair a background piece with a "point" piece. Now refer to "Making quarter square triangles" in the General Instructions.
3. "Proof" your squares to be 1-1/2" x 1-1/2".
Yield: 4. [⊠]
4. Construct the star block referring to Diagram 2. Butt seams when joining. Press seam in the direction indicated by the arrows. The block should measure 3-1/2" square.

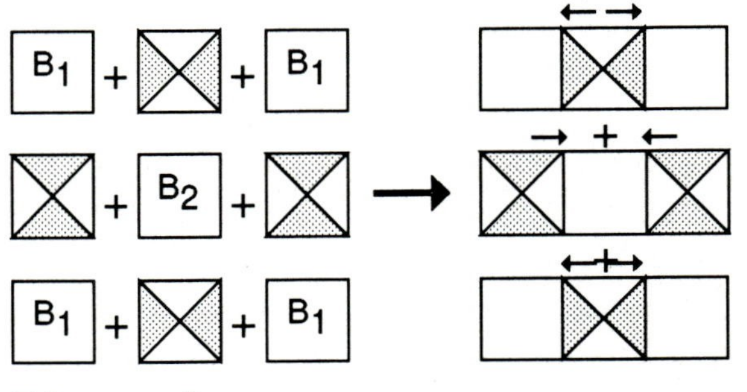

Diagram 2.

Step 2:
Triangles surrounding the center star:
1. Cut 2 squares C, 3-3/8" x 3-3/8". Sub-cut in half diagonally once.
2. Seam a triangle C to either side of the star. Press seam away from star.
3. Seam remaining triangles C to open sides of the star block. Press seam away from star. "Proof" this block to be 5" square. *Note: You will have

more than 1/4" seam allowance at the block points.

Step 3:

Sawtooth border: (makes enough at this time for use on the outer borders as well)

1. Cut one strip background 1-5/8" wide. Sub-cut into 26 squares 1-5/8" x 1-5/8". Cut one strip background fabric 1-1/4" wide. Sub-cut 4 pieces D (1-1/4" x 1-1/4"). Set the remainder of this strip aside for later use.
2. Cut one strip "sawtooth" (med./dark) fabric 1-5/8" wide. Sub-cut into 26 pieces 1-5/8" x 1-5/8".
3. Draw a diagonal line on the wrong side of all background 1-5/8" squares. Pair them up, right sides together, with "sawtooth" fabric squares. Refer to "Making half-square triangles" in the General Instructions. "Proof" the 52 squares to be 1-1/4" x 1-1/4".

Sawtooth border construction:

1. Seam the sawtooth strips according to Diagram 3. Pin and sew the "short" strips to either side of the medallion. Press according to arrows. See diagram 4.
2. Pin and sew the remaining strip with pieces D attached to them, to the open sides of the medallion. Press. Set aside the 28 remaining sawtooth blocks for later use. The block should now measure 6-1/2" x 6-1/2". See Diagram 4.

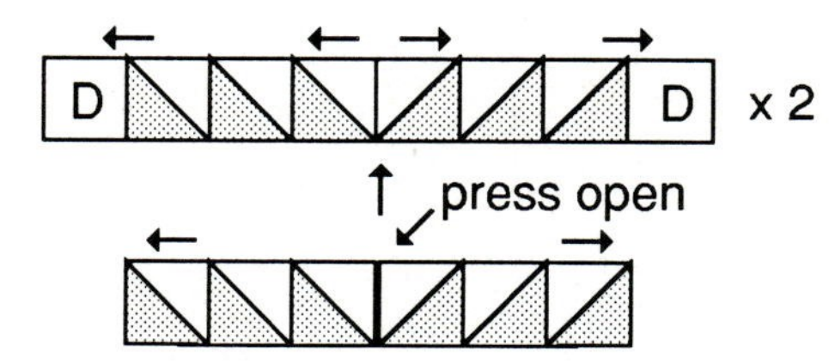

Diagram 3.

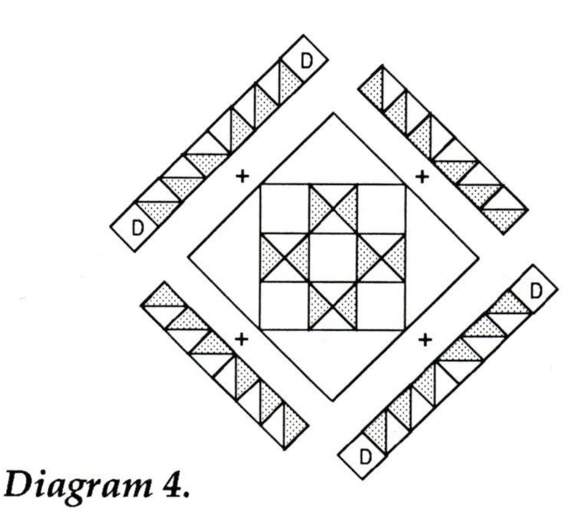

Diagram 4.

Step 4:

Triangles surrounding medallion center:

1. Cut 2 squares (dark) 5-1/8" x 5-1/8". Sub-cut the squares in half diagonally once to yield 4 pieces E.
2. Pin and sew 2 pieces E to right and left sides of the medallion. Press out.
3. Pin and sew the remaining triangles E to top and bottom of the medallion. Press out. The block should now measure 9" x 9". Refer to Whole Quilt Diagram.

Step 5:

Narrow accent border:

1. Cut one strip of accent fabric 3/4" wide. Sub-cut into: 2 pieces 3/4" x 9". Seam these strips to

right and left sides of the medallion block. Press.
2. Sub-cut 2 pieces from same strip 3/4" x 9-1/2". Seam these strips to the top and bottom of the medallion. Press. The block is now 9-1/2" x 9-1/2".

Step 6:
Adding border F: (refer to whole quilt diagram)
1. Cut 2 strips of background 1-1/4" wide.
2. For borders F, sub-cut 2 pieces 1-1/4" x 9-1/2". Pin and sew these borders to the top sand bottom of medallion. Press.

Step 7:
Adding borders G1/Sawtooth: (refer to whole quilt diagram)
1. Cut (use same fabric as used for piece C) a strip 1-1/4" wide. Sub-cut into 6 pieces 1-1/4" x 3-1/2".
2. Retrieve sawtooth blocks previously made. Piece two of the following border sections: (They should measure 2" x 9-1/2" when seamed to each other) See Diagram 5.
3. Sew borders G1/sawtooth to the top and bottom of quilt as illustrated in the Whole Quilt Diagram.

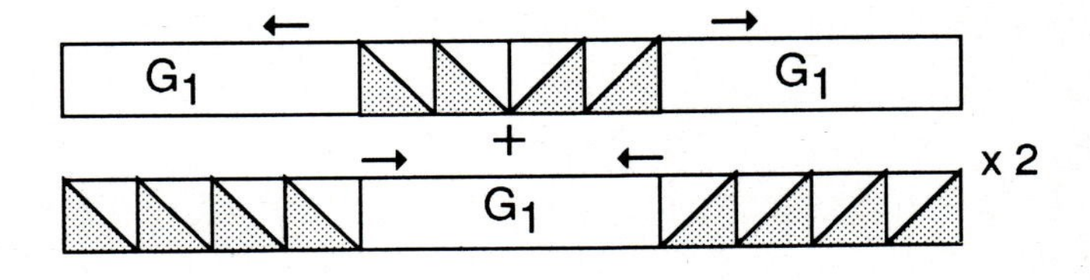

Diagram 5.

Step 8:
Adding border H: (refer to whole quilt diagram)
1. Retrieve the background strips leftover from adding border F. They are 1-1/4" wide. Sub-cut 2 pieces 1-1/4" x 12-1/2". Seam a sawtooth square to both ends of the two strips as in Diagram 6.
2. Pin and sew these H border strips to the right and the left sides of the quilt. See whole quilt diagram.

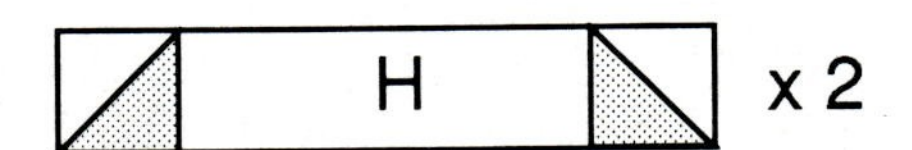

Diagram 6.

Step 9:
Adding border I: (refer to whole quilt diagram)
1. From background pre-cut 1-1/4" strip, sub-cut 4 pieces 1-1/4" x 4-1/4".
2. From same fabric as used in Step 4, cut 2 pieces 1-1/4" x 3-1/2" pieces I.
3. Piece this border strip twice as illustrated in Diagram 7. Pin and seam a border strip to the top and one to the bottom of the quilt.

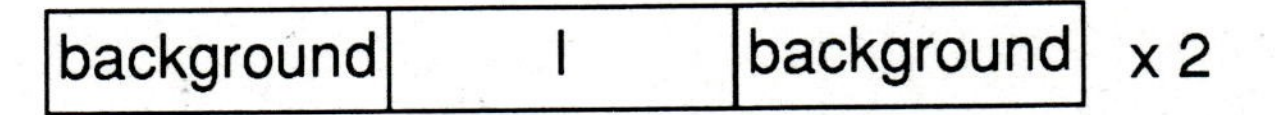

Diagram 7.

Step 10:

Final mitered border:

1. Cut 3 strips 1-1/2" wide for the inner border.
2. Cut 2 strips approximately 2-1/2" wide (striped or other) and at least 25" long for outer border side strips and 2 strips approximately 2-1/2" wide and at least 22" long for top and bottom borders. **Note:* If you are using a striped border fabric, please cut 4 pieces having exactly the same pattern repeat and width.
3. Cut 1 of the inner border strips in half. Pair these strips with the 22" long outer border strips. Seam one inner border strip to one outer border strip along the long edge. Press. Repeat for the other 2 strips.
4. Pair the remaining 2 inner border strips with remaining outer border strips. Seam one inner border strip to one outer border strip along the long edge. Press. Repeat for the other 2 strips.
5. Refer to General Instructions for "Mitered borders".

Step 11:

Finishing the quilt:

Refer to the whole quilt diagram and the General Instructions for marking quilting lines, batting up the quilt, quilting, and binding.

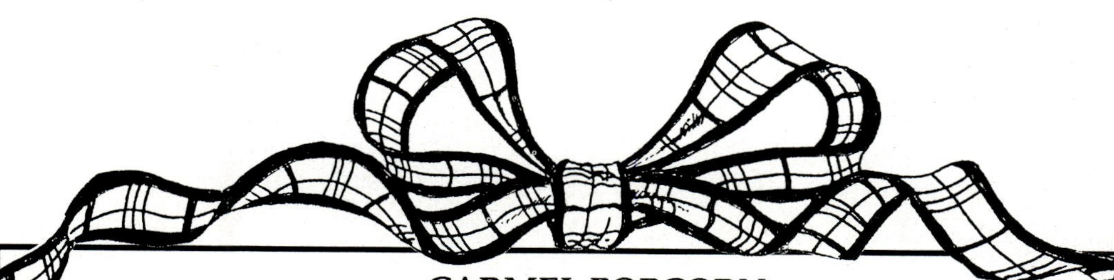

CARMEL POPCORN

A great small gift for kids!

2 bags "Hul-less" popcorn
1 stick margarine (melted)
2 cups packed brown sugar
1 teaspoon salt
1/2 cup dark Karo syrup
1 teaspoon baking soda
1 teaspoon vanilla flavoring
1 cup roasted, salted peanuts (optional)

—Mix together margarine, sugar, salt, and syrup in a microwave bowl. Microwave for 5 minutes - mixture will be boiling. Add the soda and vanilla - the mixture will foam.

—Put popcorn in large roasting pan - pour syrup over popcorn. Add peanuts if desired. Bake in a 200° oven for 1 hour; stirring every 10 minutes.

—Carmel popcorn stores well in an airtight tin. For gift baskets or small gifts, fill a cellophane bag and tie it up with brightly colored ribbons.

Zig Zag Quilt

finished size: 29" x 36"

Wallhanging/table runner - approximately 29" x 36"
(Quick-cutting and piecing instructions only)
Block size: finished 5-1/4" x 5-1/4"
Number of blocks: 11 whole blocks, 2 half blocks
Setting: diagonal, zig-zag
Pre-wash all fabric. This is a scrap quilt. Different fabrics were used for each block as well as for the setting triangles and corner triangles.

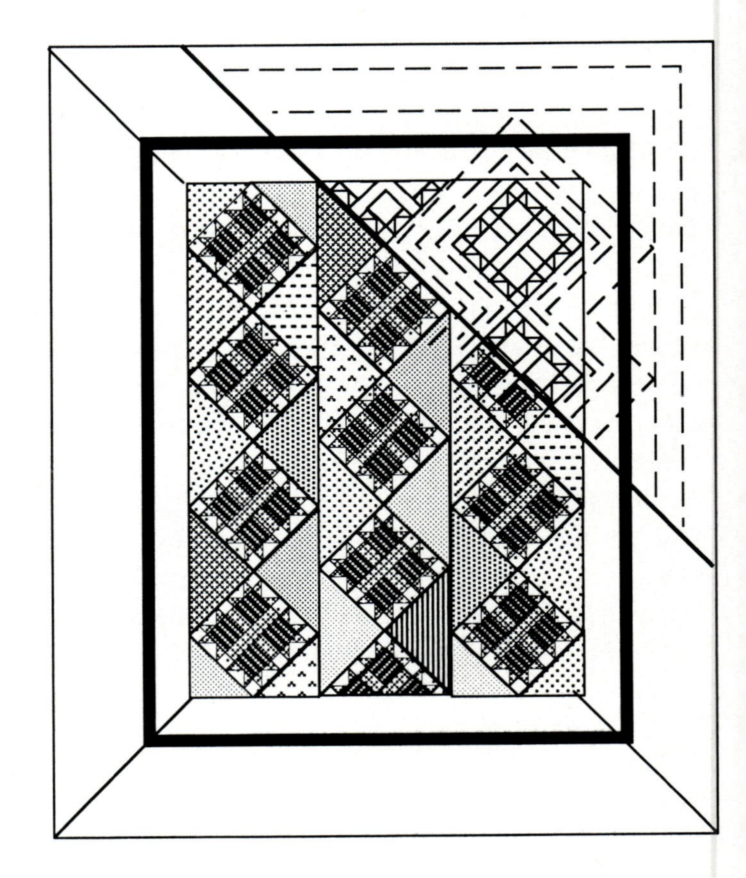

Fabric requirements:
—Scraps of light, medium, medium/dark, and dark value fabrics for pieced blocks
—Larger scraps for the inset triangles (at least 8-3/4" x 5" - 20 or so)
—1st border: 1/4 yard
—2nd border: 1/8 yard
—3rd border: 1/2 yard
—Binding: 1/4 yard
—Backing and batting: 1 yard of each

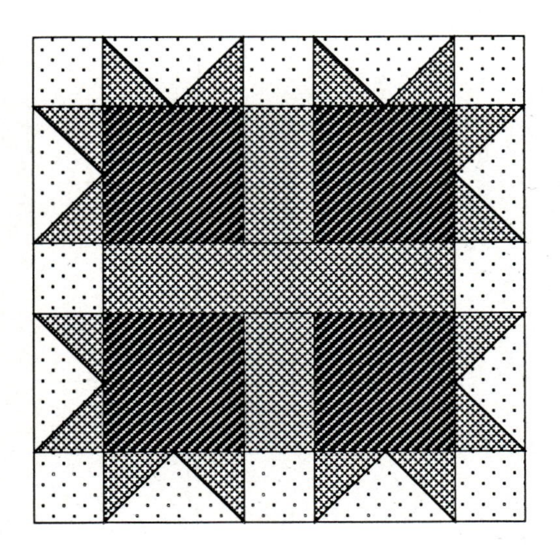

Whole Block

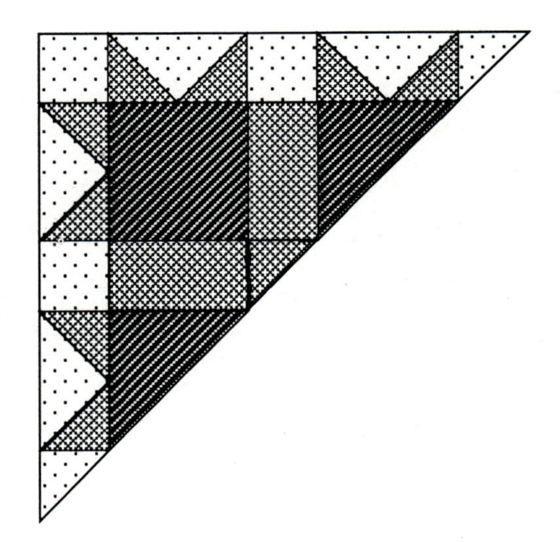

Half Block

Cutting instructions for the "whole" block: 11 blocks required.
Cutting is for *one* block:
Background: 8 - 1-1/4" x 1-1/4" (B1), 8 - 1-1/4" x 2" (C1)
Bright value fabric: (points and cross) 16 - 1-1/4" x 1-1/4" (B2), 2 - 1-1/4" x 2" (C2), 1 - 1-1/4" x 4-1/4" (F)
Medium/dark fabric: (4 corner squares) 4 - 2" x 2" (A1)

Cutting instructions for the "half" block: 2 blocks required.
Cutting is for *one* block:
Background: 1 -1-5/8" x 1-5/8" square. Sub-cut in half diagonally once (D). 3 - 1-1/4" x 1-1/4" (B1), 4 - 1-1/4" x 2" (C1)
Bright value fabric: (points and crosses) 8 - 1-1/4" x 1-1/4" (B2), 2 - 1-1/4" x 2" (C2). 1 - 1-5/8" x 1-5/8". Sub-cut in half diagonally once (E). (only need one.)
Medium/dark fabric: (corner blocks) 1 - 2" x 2" (A), 1 - 2-3/8" x 2-3/8". Sub-cut in half diagonally once to yield 2 triangles (G).

Piecing the "whole" block:
For *one* block:
1. Retrieve the 8 background C rectangles and the 16 point fabric squares B2. Draw a diagonal line on the wrong side of all the squares. Refer to General Instructions under "Making double half-square triangles". Follow the instructions carefully. "Proof" (see General Instructions) your pieces to be 1-1/4" x 2". 

x 8

2. Assemble block according to Diagram 1. Make 4 of the units shown in the diagram. The arrows show pressing direction.

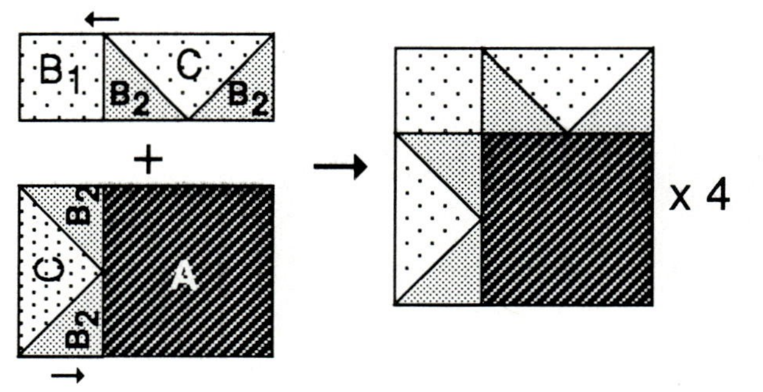

Diagram 1.

3. Make 2 sections following Diagram 2.

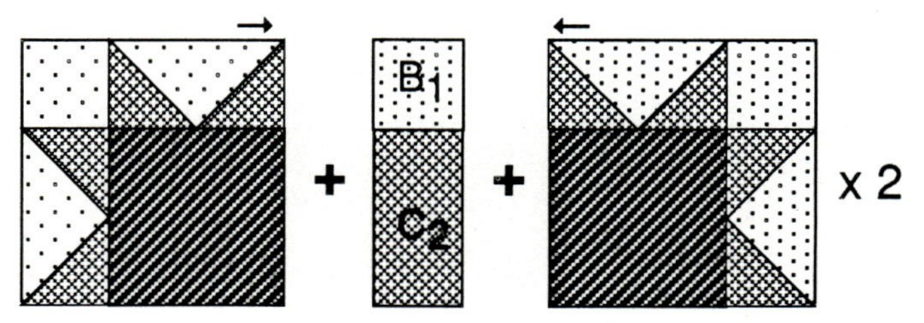

Diagram 2.

4. Pin and stitch sections together, butting seams. The blocks should measure 5-3/4" x 5-3/4". See Diagram 3.
5. Repeat procedure for the other 10 blocks.

Piecing the half-blocks: 2 required
For *one* block:
1. Retrieve 4 background rectangles C1 and the 8 point fabric squares B2. Refer to #1 under "Piecing whole blocks" and make 4 

double half-square triangle units.
2. Assemble the block as in Diagram 4.

Cutting inset triangles and corners:
1. Use templates 1 and 2 for cutting triangle insets and corners. (**Note:** if you are using only a few different background fabrics you may cut an 8-3/4" square for the inset triangles. Sub-cut in half diagonally twice to yield 4 inset triangles of the same fabric ☒.)
2. Cut 20 inset triangles (Template 1) paying close attention to the straight of the fabric. Cut 8 corner triangles using Template 2.

Quilt layout:
1. Lay out the quilt in a pleasing manner, referring to whole quilt diagram. The quilt is assembled in three strip units. Pin and stitch each strip carefully. Pin and stitch the strips together. See Diagram 5.
2. Add corners last.

Bordering the quilt:
1. First border: Cut 4 strips 1-1/4" wide.
   Second border: Cut 4 strips 3/4" wide.
   Third border: Cut 4 strips 3-1/4" wide.
   Binding: Cut 4 strips 2-1/4" wide.
2. Sew a first border strip to a second border strip to a third border strip. Press carefully to one side. Repeat for the other three border strips.
3. Refer to "Mitered borders" in the General Instructions.

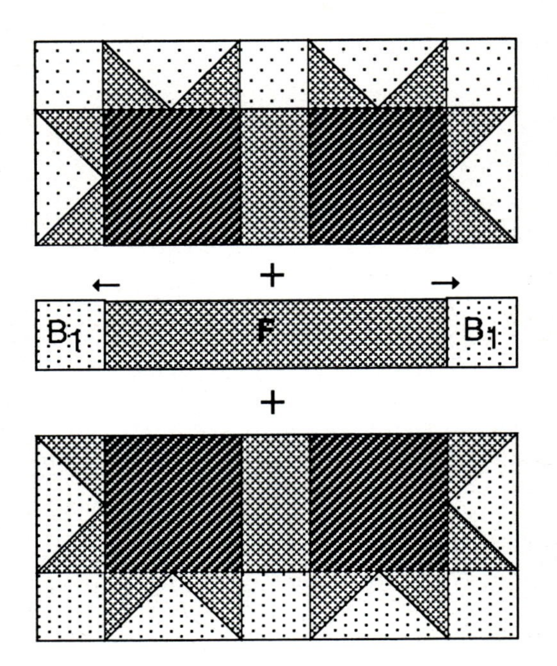

Diagram 3.

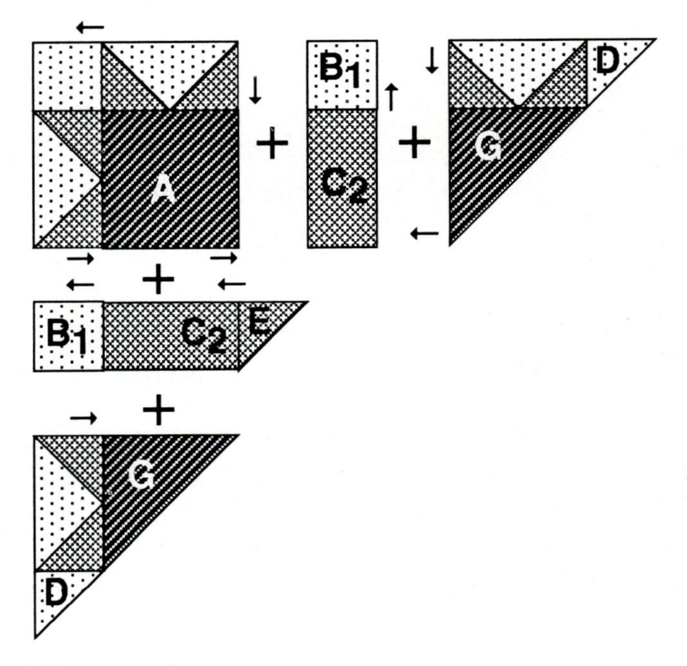

Diagram 4.

Marking quilting lines:

Mark quilting lines according to quilting diagram on whole quilt diagram.

Finishing:

Refer to General Instructions for layering up the quilt, hand or machine quilting, and binding the quilt.

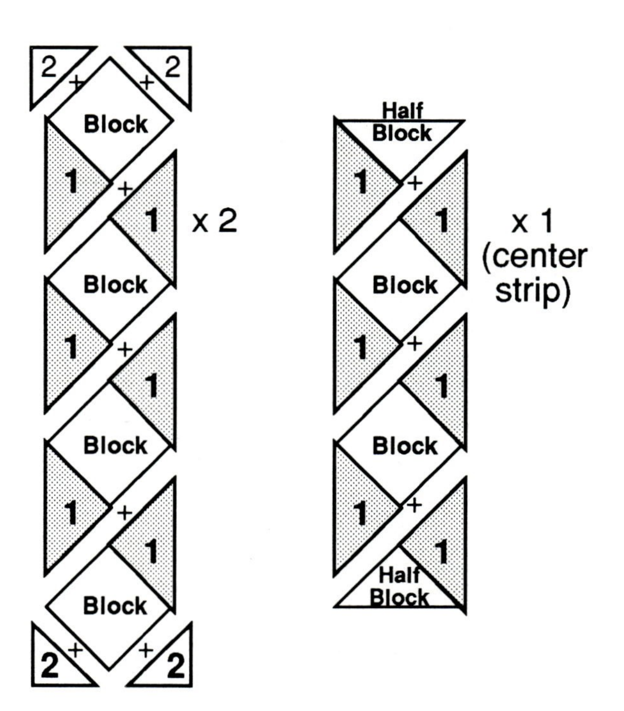

Diagram 5.

LEMON NUT BREAD WITH CITRUS GLAZE

makes one 9 x 5 inch loaf

1/2 cup butter or margarine (softened)
1 cup sugar
2 large eggs
Grated peel of one lemon, about 1 teaspoon, packed
1-1/2 cups all-purpose flour
1 teaspoon baking powder
1/2 teaspoon salt
1/2 cup chopped nuts, preferably walnuts
1/2 cup milk
Glaze: Juice of one lemon
1/2 cup confectioners' sugar

— Heat oven to 350°. Grease 9 x 5 x 3-inch bread pan. In large bowl of electric mixer, beat butter and sugar at medium speed until light and fluffy. Beat in all remaining ingredients, except glaze ingredients, in order given. Pour batter into prepared pan and bake 45-55 minutes until wooden pick inserted near center of loaf comes out clean. Remove bread from oven and cool in pan on wire rack about 15 minutes.

— Meanwhile, stir lemon juice into confectioners' sugar in small bowl until sugar is dissolved and mixture is smooth. Remove bread from pan and place on rack. After setting rack on waxed paper to catch drips, spoon glaze over warm bread. Cool completely before slicing.

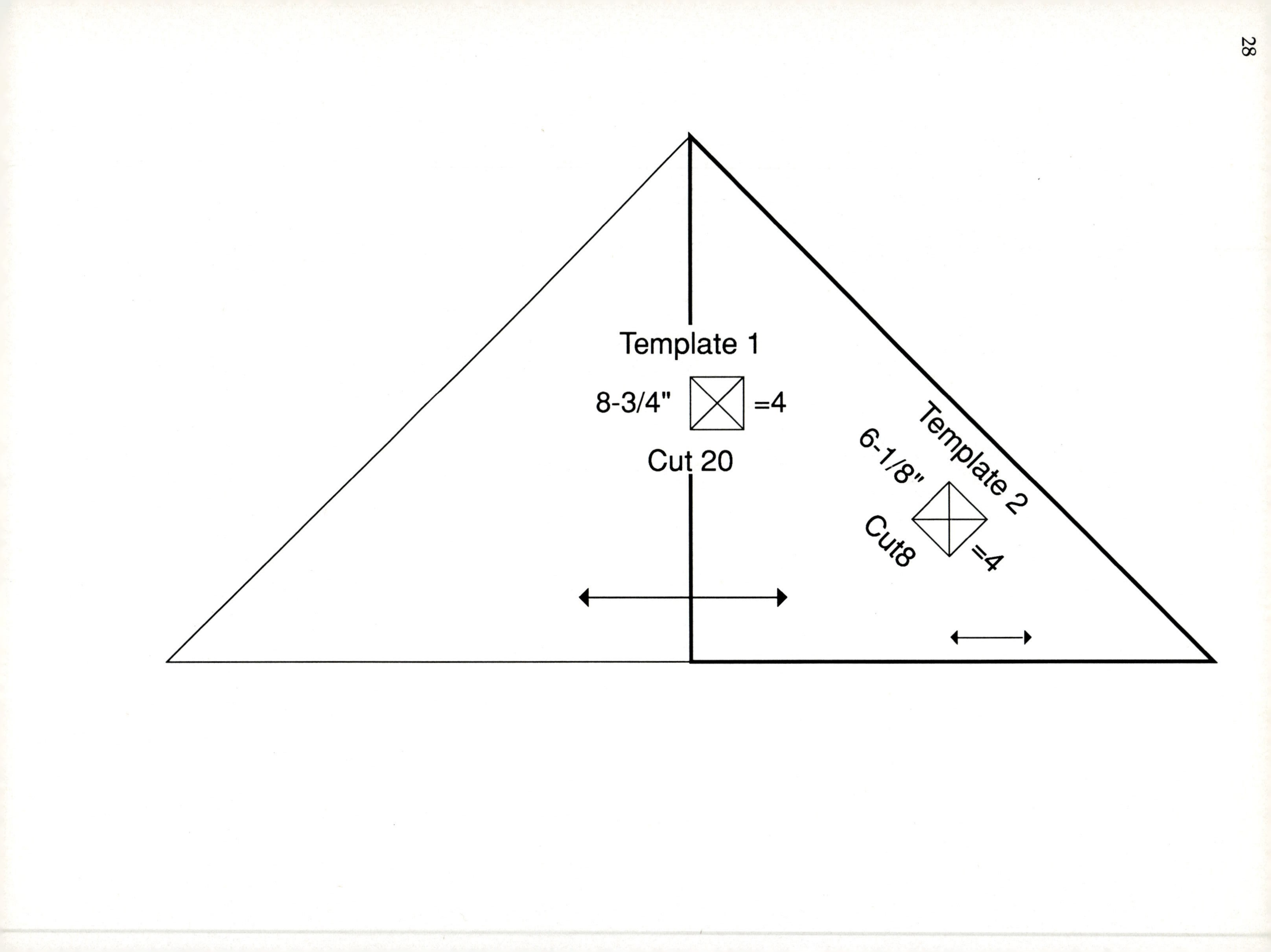
Template 1
8-3/4"
=4
Cut 20
Template 2
6-1/8"
=4
Cut8

Mini Sampler

finished size: 15" x 19"

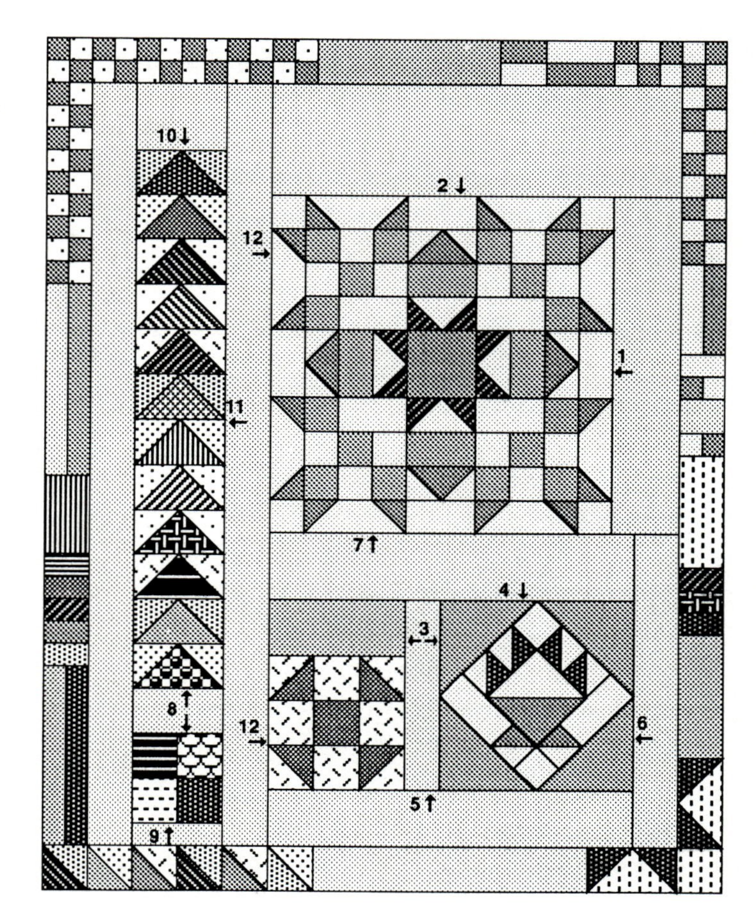

Fabric requirements:
— Scraps of various backgrounds (lights), mediums, medium/darks, and darks
— 1/4 yd. lattice
—1/4 yds. binding
— 1/2 yd. batting and backing

Block 1: Starburst - unfinished size 8" x 8"
Cutting instructions:
From background:
Cut 2 strips 1-1/4" wide, then sub-cut:
1. 24 pieces A1 (1-1/4" x 1-1/4")
2. 8 pieces B (1-1/4" x 2-3/4")
3. 12 pieces F1 (1-1/4" x 2")

From center star points:
1. 8 pieces A2 (1-1/4" x 1-1/4")

From accent color (also star center):
1. 1 piece H (2" x 2")
2. One strip 1-1/4" wide, then sub-cut into 16 pieces A3 (1-1/4" x 1-1/4") for points, and 4 pieces F2 (1-1/4" x 2")

Fourth color (checkerboard):
1. Cut 16 pieces A (1-1/4" x 1-1/4")
2. 4 pieces F3 (1-1/4" x 2")

Starburst construction:
1. Retrieve 8 background pieces B (1-1/4" x 2-3/4") and 16 pieces A3 (1-1/4" x 1-1/4") of accent color.
2. Draw a diagonal line ⧅ on the back of all A3 pieces . Place 2 A3 pieces, right sides together, on opposite corners of B piece. Stitch on the pre-marked lines. Now trim down the seam allowance to 1/4". Open out A3 pieces and press. Repeat this entire procedure for the other seven B pieces. See Diagram.
3. Assemble F2A1 sections. Retrieve 4 F2 (1-1/4" x 2") of accent fabric and 8 A1 (1-1/4" x 1-1/4") of background fabric. Draw a diagonal line ⧅ on the wrong side of all A1 squares. Now refer to "Making double half-square triangles" as explained in the General Instructions at the front of this book.
4. Assemble F1A2 sections for inner star. Re-

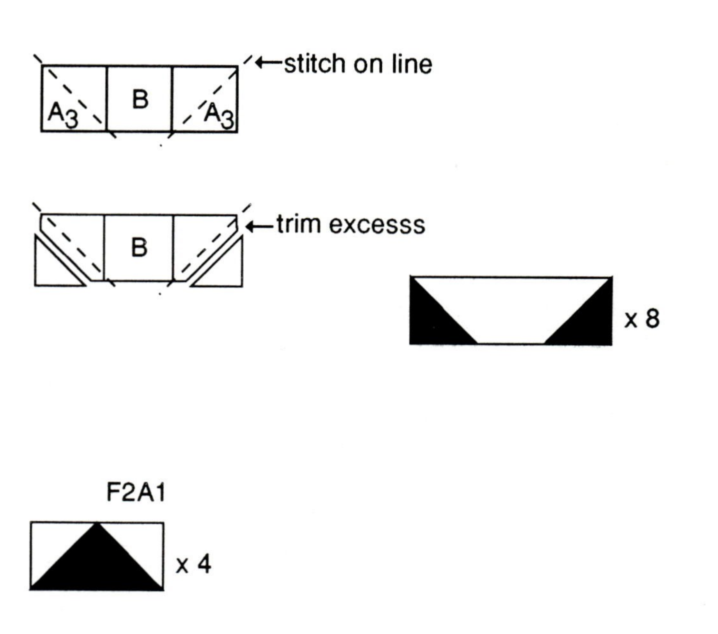

trieve 4 F1 (1-1/4" x 2") of background and 8 A2 (1-1/4" x 1-1/4") of star point fabric. Draw a diagonal line on the wrong side of all pieces A2. Refer to General Instructions for "Making double half-square triangles".

5. Now follow the piecing diagram for assembling the entire unit. Piece Unit 1 twice. Join Unit 1 to 2, to Unit 1. Follow arrow direction for pressing.

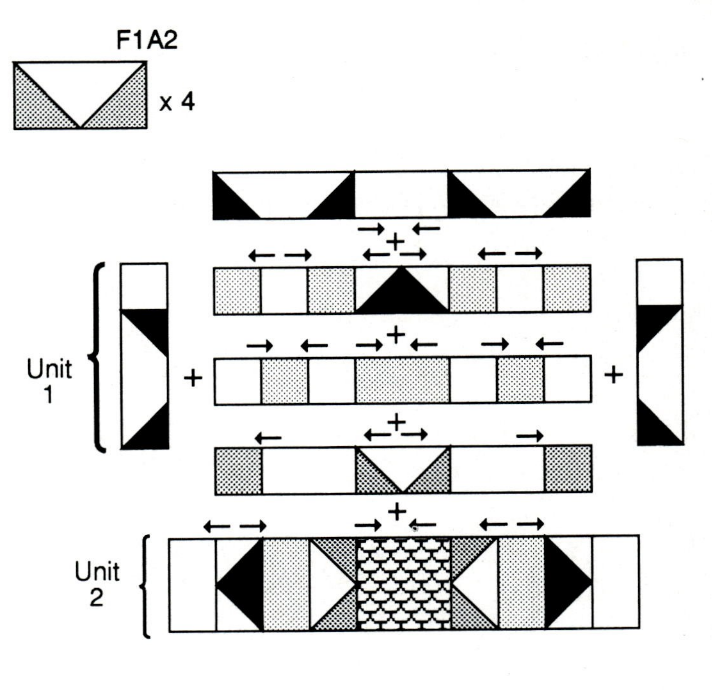

Block 2: Shoo-fly - unfinished size 3-1/2" x 3-1/2"

Cutting instructions:

From background:

1. 2 pieces C1 (1-7/8" x 1-7/8")
2. 4 pieces D1 (1-1/2" x 1-1/2")

From dark:

1. 2 pieces C2 (1-7/8" x 1-7/8")
2. 1 piece D2 (1-1/2" x 1-1/2")

Shoo-fly construction:

1. Draw a diagonal line on the wrong side of the background pieces C1 . Pair them with dark pieces C2. Follow the General Instructions for "Making half-square triangles". "Proof" your blocks to 1-1/2" x 1-1/2". (See General Instructions for proofing).
2. Follow the piecing diagram for block construction. Arrows show the direction for pressing.
3. Cut and stitch 1-3/4" x 3-1/2" strip of fabric to the side of the finished block.

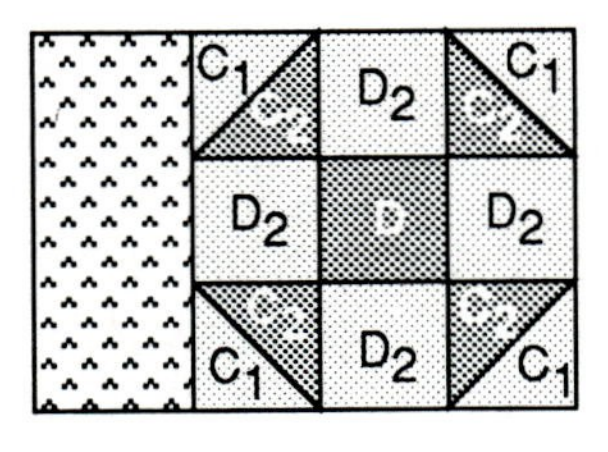

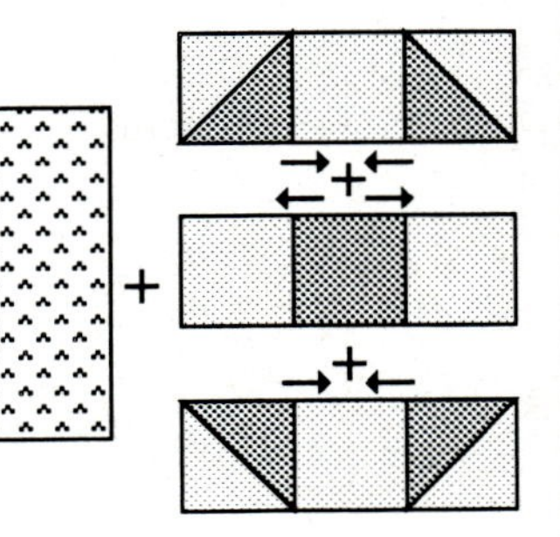

Block 3: Cake Stand - unfinished size 4-3/4" x 4-3/4"

Cutting instructions:

From background:

1. 2 pieces A (1-1/4" x 1-1/4")
2. 3 pieces B1 (1-5/8" x 1-5/8")
3. 2 pieces F (1-1/4" x 2")
4. 1 piece E1 (2-3/8" x 2-3/8")

From basket top fabric:

1. 2 pieces B2 (1-5/8" x 1-5/8")

From basket base fabric:

1. 1 piece E2 (2-3/8" x 2-3/8")
2. 1 piece B3 (1-5/8" x 1-5/8")

From outer triangle fabric:

1. 2 pieces G (3" x 3"). Sub-cut these squares in

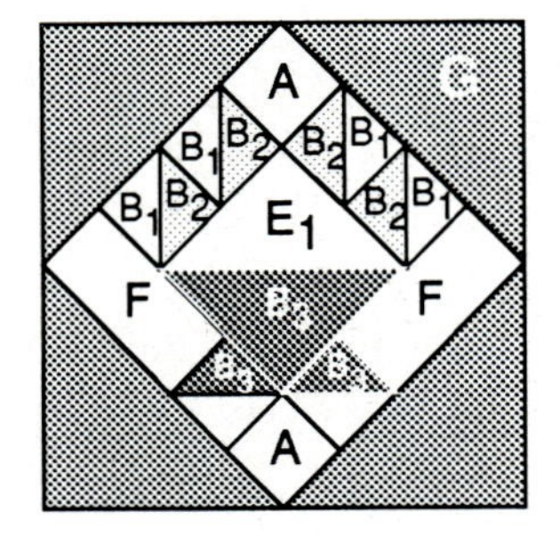

half diagonally once to yield 4 triangles.

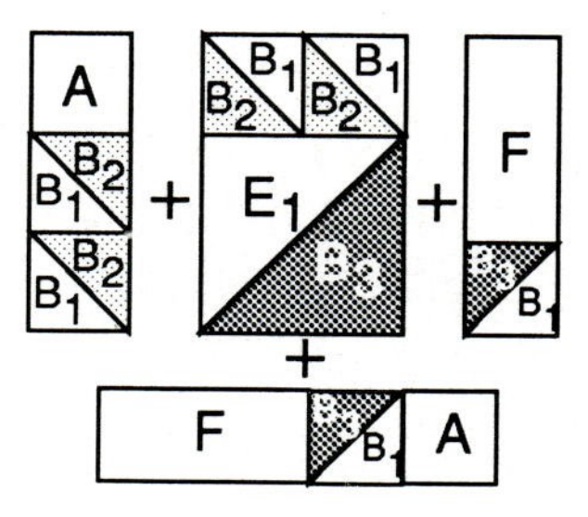

Cake stand construction:

1. Draw a diagonal line on the wrong side of the 3 background pieces B1. Place these pieces right sides together with the basket top pieces B2 (2) and the one basket base square B3. Refer to "Making half-square triangles" in the General Instructions. "Proof" these squares to be 1-1/4" square.
2. Draw a diagonal line on the wrong side of piece E1 of background. Place this piece, right sides together, with piece E2 of basket base fabric. Repeat "Making half-square triangles" procedure. "Proof" this square to be 2" square. You only need one of these blocks.
3. Follow the diagram for block construction.
4. Stitch the 2 triangles G to either side of the finished block. Press out. Stitch the two remaining G's to opposite sides. Press out.

Block 4: Flying geese - unfinished size of one block: 1-1/2" x 2-1/2". Unit of 12 blocks required. The following instructions are for a single block:
From background: 2 pieces D (1-1/2" x 1-1/2")
From darker fabric: 1 piece N (1-1/2" x 2-1/2")

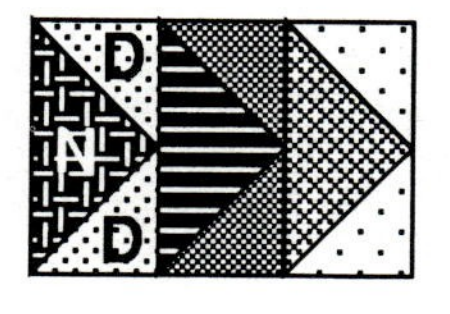

Flying geese construction:

1. Draw a diagonal line on the wrong side of pieces D (1-1/2" square). Now follow directions for making double half-square triangles as written in the General Instructions. Proof block to be 1-1/2" x 2-1/2".

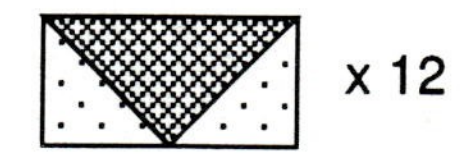

Block 5: Four patch - unfinished size 2-1/2" x 2-1/2"

Cutting instructions:
From background: 2 pieces K1 (1-1/2" x 1-1/2")
From dark: 2 pieces K2 (1-1/2" x 1-1/2")

Four patch assembly:

1. Stitch a K1 to K2. Repeat with other 2 pieces. Press light towards dark.
2. Stitch together units, butting seams.

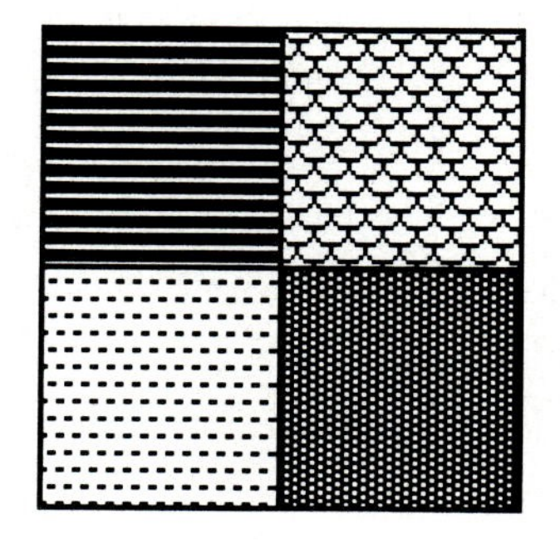

Lattice stripping:
Cutting instructions:

Cut 1 strip 3" wide, 1 strip 1-3/4" wide, and 1 strip 1-1/2" wide. Sub-cut the following pieces from the pre-cut strips: ***Note:* It is helpful to number the lattice pieces as you cut. The exact measurements for each strip are under #4.

1. From the 3" strip cut Lattice #2. Trim strip to 2" wide. Cut Lattice #1, 4, and 10.
2. From the 1-3/4" wide strip cut Lattice #5. Trim the remaining strip down to 1-1/2" wide. Cut Lattices #6 and 8. Trim strip down to 1" wide. Cut Lattice #9.
3. From the 1-1/2" wide strip cut 2 Lattices #11. Trim the remainder down to 1-1/4" wide. Cut #3.
4. Follow the corresponding Lattice Numbers with the numbers on the diagram of the Sampler quilt. The lattices must be sewn in the numerical order as given 1-11.

#1	2" x 8"	#7	Join
#2	3" x 9-1/2"	#8	1-1/2" x 2-1/2"
#3	1-1/4" x 4-3/4"	#9	1" x 2-1/2"
#4	2" x 8-1/2"	#10	2" x 2-1/2"
#5	1-3/4" x 8-1/2"	#11	1-1/2"x17-1/2" (2)
#6	1-1/2" x 7-1/2"	#12	Join

Pieced Borders:

Left Border:

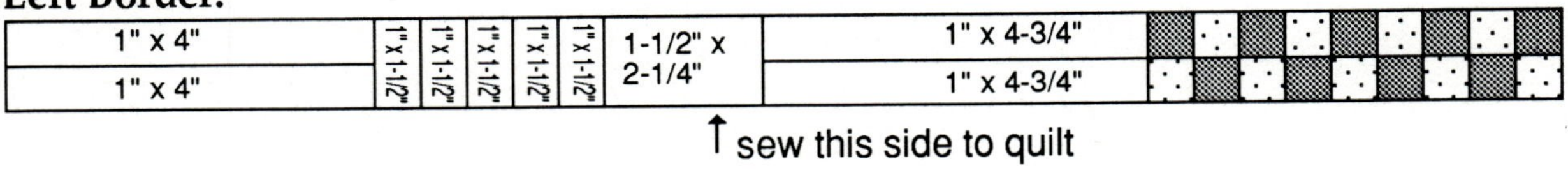

1" x 4"
1" x 4"
1" x 1-1/2"
1" x 1-1/2"
1" x 1-1/2"
1" x 1-1/2"
1" x 1-1/2"
1-1/2" x 2-1/4"
1" x 4-3/4"
1" x 4-3/4"
sew this side to quilt

1. Strip section - Follow the diagram above, cutting the strips from various scrap fabrics. The measurements for the strip sizes include the seam allowance. Sew each section to border as completed. (For fabric variations, see colored photo.)
2. Checkerboard section - Cut one strip each of a dark and a light fabric 1" wide. Sub-cut the strips in half (along the short side).
3. Sew one light to one dark strip. Press light to dark carefully, don't pull the fabric out of shape. Sub-cut this strip section into 21 pieces at 1" intervals.
4. Join the pieces back together to make 2 checkerboard strips. One strip is 9 units and the other is 12 units (set this 12 unit aside for top border). Sew the completed 9 unit checkerboard to the left border strip.

Right Border:

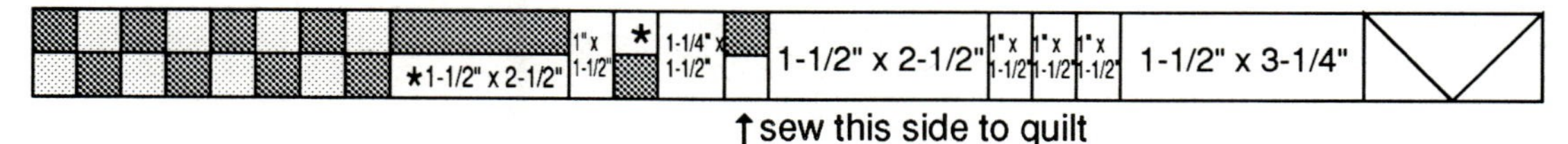

1. Checkerboard section - Cut 1 strip each of a light and a dark fabric 1" wide.
2. Stitch strips together along the long edge, right sides together. Press light towards dark. Sub-cut this strip section into 15 pieces at 1" intervals. Sew 8 of these units together for now, and set 2 aside for later use in this border. (The remaining 5 pieces will be used in making the top border.) Also cut the following from the remainder of this strip section: one *1-1/2" x 2-1/2", one *1-1/2" x 2", and one *1-1/2" x 1-1/2". The 1-1/2" x 2-1/2" piece will be used in the * for the right border. Set the others aside for use in the top border.
3. Strip section: Follow the diagram for the right border, cutting various strips from scrap fabrics. The measurements for the strip sizes include the seam allowances. The starred units have already been cut previously from checkerboard strip. Sew each section to the border as completed.
4. Flying geese - Cut 2 pieces of background (1-1/2" x 2-1/2"). Cut 4 pieces from med./dark fabric (1-1/2" square). Follow the directions for making "Double half-square triangles" in General Instructions. Add one unit to the end of the border strip. Set the other aside for later use in the bottom border.

Top Border -

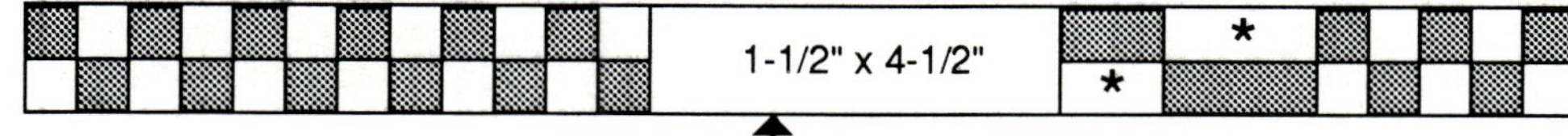

1. Retrieve the checkerboard unit made with the left border. Retrieve the checkerboard unit and the starred pieces cut while making the right border.
2. Strip section - Follow the diagram for top border using the pre-assembled checkerboard sections, starred sections, and various cut scrap pieces complete the border.

Bottom Border -

1. Make "Half-square triangles" - Cut 1 square (1-7/8") from each of three different background fabrics. Cut 1 square (1-7/8") from each of three different med./dark fabrics. Refer to General Instructions for "Making half-square triangles". "Proof" finished squares to 1-1/2". Yield: 6.
2. Retrieve the pre-assembled double half-square triangles (flying geese block) previously made.
3. Assemble the border according to diagram. For the strip section cut scraps to indicated dimensions.

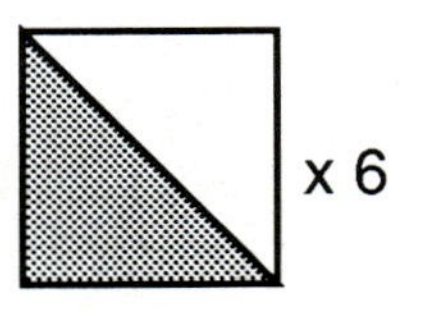

Finishing the quilt -
1. Press all borders. Sew side borders on first. Press out. Sew top and bottom borders on. Press.
2. Mark quilting lines.
3. Cut 2 strips 2-1/4" wide for binding. Cut batting and backing 18" x 22".
4. Refer to General Instructions for batting up the quilt, machine or hand quilting, quilting, and binding.

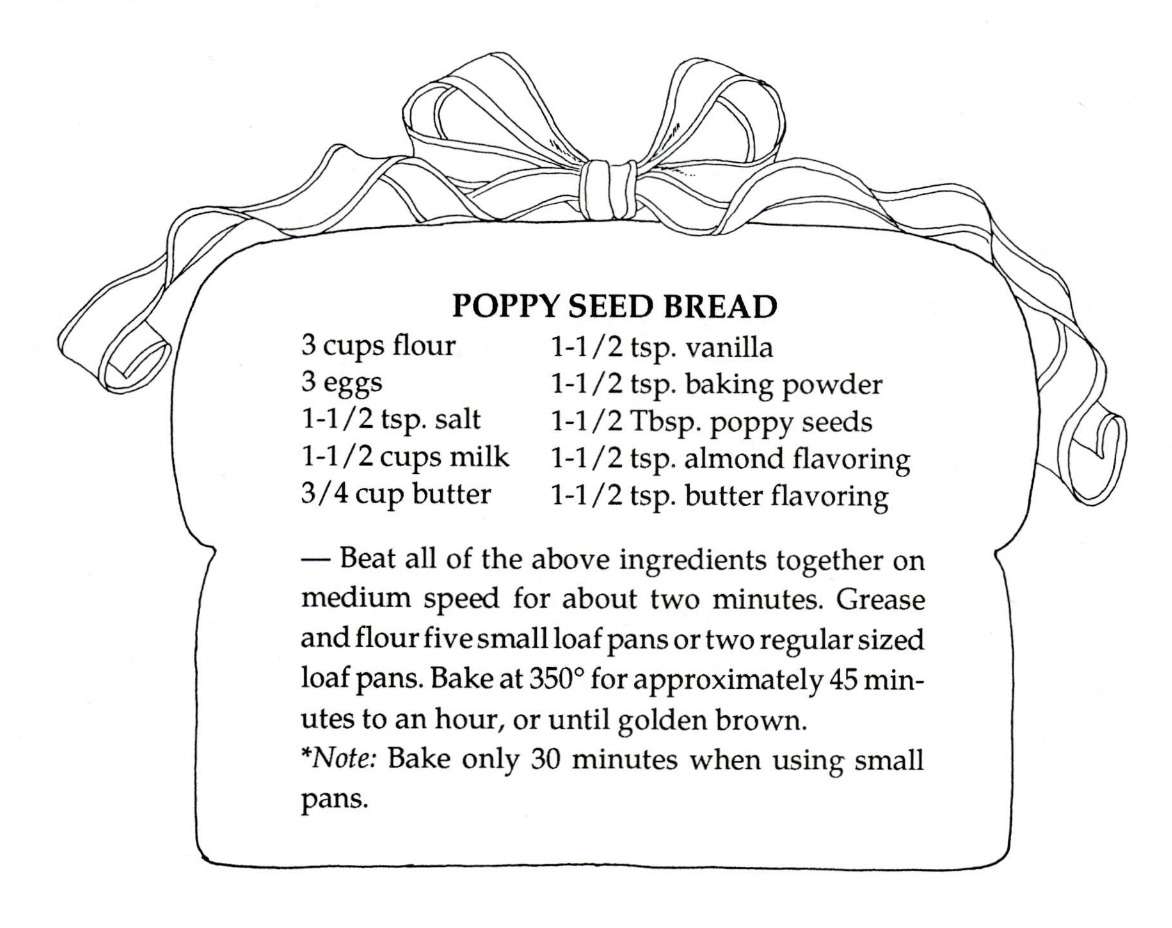

POPPY SEED BREAD

3 cups flour	1-1/2 tsp. vanilla
3 eggs	1-1/2 tsp. baking powder
1-1/2 tsp. salt	1-1/2 Tbsp. poppy seeds
1-1/2 cups milk	1-1/2 tsp. almond flavoring
3/4 cup butter	1-1/2 tsp. butter flavoring

— Beat all of the above ingredients together on medium speed for about two minutes. Grease and flour five small loaf pans or two regular sized loaf pans. Bake at 350° for approximately 45 minutes to an hour, or until golden brown.
**Note:* Bake only 30 minutes when using small pans.

Framed Mini Quilts

Framed Starburst

Framed size:14-1/4" x 14-1/4"

1. Refer to cutting instructions and construction under *Block 1:* Starburst, under **Mini Sampler.**
2. Follow instructions exactly. After the block is made you need to add a mitered border of stripped fabric. Decide how wide you want your border to be. Add another 2" to that measurement to allow for folding the excess to the back of the mat board. For instance: I want my border to be 2-1/2" finished. I added 2" to that amount (3") and cut my border strips 5" wide. Therefore, my border strips had to be cut no less than 5" x 18". (The actual length of my picture side is approximately 16-1/2". A few inches are added because of mitering.)
3. Cut the 4 border strips from the same stripe in the border fabric.
4. Miter border on according to "Mitered borders" in the General Instructions. ** *NOTE:* if the same design on the border strip is centered in the exact center of the quilt block on all four sides, the corner designs should match up nicely.
5. Refer to Diagram 1 for quilting suggestions. Refer to General Instructions for layering up the quilt block and machine or hand quilting.
6. Have the block professionally framed or do it yourself.

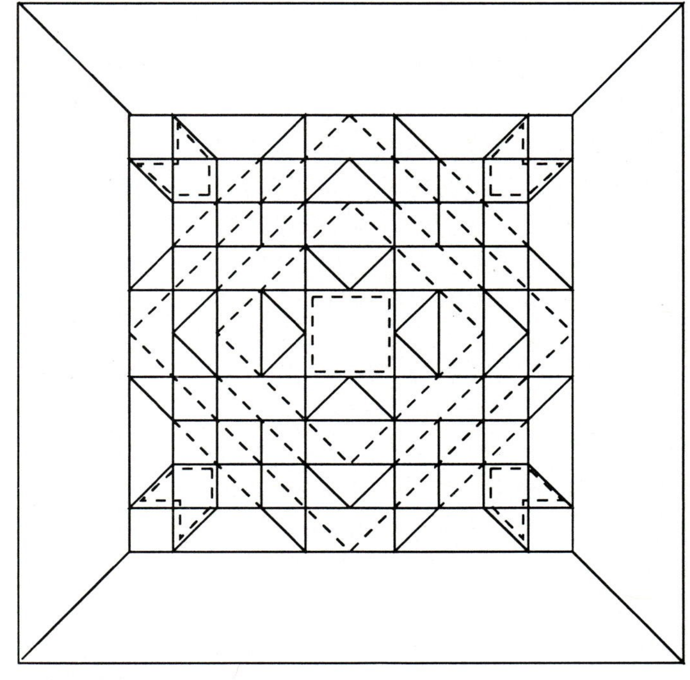

Diagram 1.

Framed Shoo-fly Block

Framed size: 8-1/2" x 8-1/2"

1. Refer to cutting instructions and construction for the Shoo-fly block, *Block 2*, under **Mini Sampler.** *Omit #3 under construction.
2. Cut 1 strip 3/4" wide from an "accent" fabric for inner border. Cut 1 strip 4" wide from fabric for the outer border.
3. Seam both borders on according to "Bordering a quilt" instructions under General Instructions. The quilt block has an excessive outer border for ease in folding the fabric to the back of the mat board.
4. Refer to Diagram 1 for quilting suggestions. Refer to General Instructions for layering up the quilt block and machine or hand quilting.
5. This particular picture was matted professionally. Only 1/2" of the outer boarder actually shows. The finished framed picture is 8-1/2" x 8-1/2".

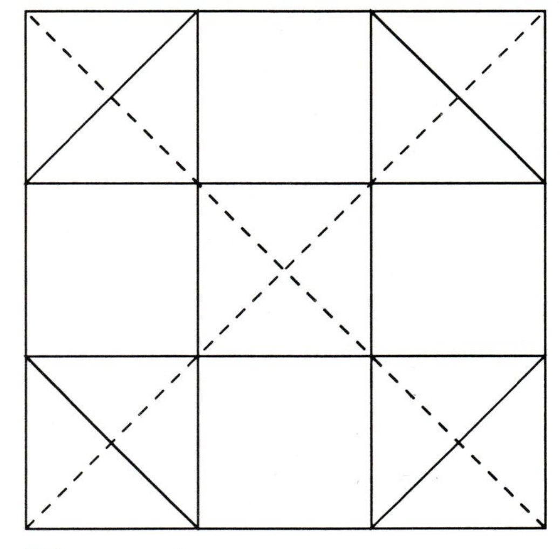
Diagram 1.

Framed Cake stand, Flying geese, and Checkerboard

Framed size: 8-1/2" x 10-1/4"

1. Refer to cutting instructions and construction under *Block 3:* Cake stand, under **Mini Sampler.** Make the block and set aside.
2. Refer to cutting instructions and construction under *Block 4,* Flying geese, under **Mini Sampler**. Make 4 flying geese blocks. Stitch the flying geese blocks together vertically. See Diagram 3. Cut 1 accent strip 3/4" x 18". Sub-cut into 2 pieces 3/4" x 4-1/2" and 2 pieces 3/4" x 3". Carefully seam the side pieces (3/4" x 4-1/2") on first. Press. Seam top and bottom (3/4" x 3") to unit. Press. Set aside.
3. To make Checkerboard strip: Cut 1 dark and 1 light strip 1" x 12". Seam, right sides together, along one long edge. Press carefully so the strip doesn't ripple. Press light towards dark. Sub-cut this strip section into 9 pieces at 1" intervals. Join the pieces together, butting seams, to make a checkerboard strip. See Diagram 3. Press. Set aside.
4. Lattice stripping: (3/8 yard required) Lattice strips are cut and sewn on in numerical order: (refer to Diagram 3)

#1 3/4" x 4-3/4"
#2 1" x 4-3/4"
#3 1" x 5-1/2"
#4 3/4" x 1-1/2"
#5 Join checkerboard to cake stand block
#6 3/4" x 3"
#7 1-3/4" x 3"
#8 Join flying geese to other section
#9 2 - 3" x 6-3/4"
#10 2 - 3" x length of piece

5. Mark quilting lines if necessary. Refer to General Instructions for layering up the quilt block and machine or hand quilting.
6. Have the block professionally framed or frame it yourself.

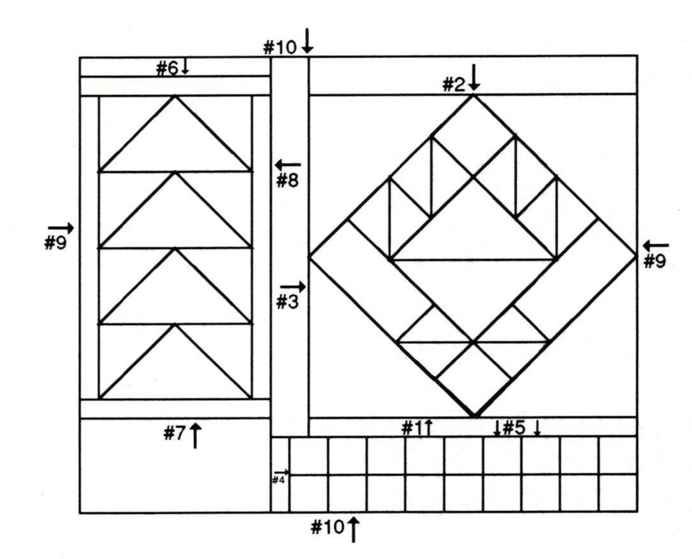

Diagram 3.

Medallion Quilt

finished size 45" x 45"

Due to the nature of a medallion style quilt, it is very difficult to anticipate the purchase of border fabrics, and the like, before you begin sewing. I would suggest selecting one fabric - a plaid, large floral, etc., and building your fabric selections around that one fabric. Try to incorporate accent, background, medium value, and dark value fabrics in your quilt. Vary the scale or size of your fabrics. Include tiny prints, plaids, large florals, and overall designs in order to give your quilt life. Yardage for the medallion quilt is as accurate as possible due to the fact that many "scraps" were used.

Medallion Whole Quilt Diagram.

Fabric and supply requirements:

—Background for center star unit: 1/4 yd.

—Star points for center star unit: scraps of 4 medium/ dark fabrics

—Star centers for center star unit: scraps of 1 medium fabric

—Accent strip around center star unit: 1/8 yd.

—Large triangles around center star unit: 2 - 9" x 9" squares

—Dark accent border (used 3 times for borders) and binding: 3/4 yd.

—Sawtooth background: 5" wide strip

—Sawtooth dark and first border: 3/8 yd. med./ dark

—Border between sawtooth and windmills: 1/4 yd.

—Windmills: scraps of 5 backgrounds and 5 medium to medium/dark fabrics

—Setting fabric around windmills: 3/8 yd. of medium/light fabric

—Inset triangles around windmills: 5/8 yd. of medium fabric

—Outer border: 1/2 yd.

—Backing: 1-3/8 yds.

—Batting: 48" x 48"

—Template plastic

Center star block unit: unfinished size 12-1/2" x 12-1/2"

Cutting instructions:

Background:

1. Cut 1 strip 2" wide. Sub-cut into 12 - 2" x 3-1/2" pieces B1
2. Cut 1 strip 2-5/8" wide. Sub-cut into 4 - 2-5/8"

x 2-5/8" pieces D, and 4 - 2" x 2" pieces A1.

Star points: 4 different medium/dark to dark

1. Cut 2 pieces 2-3/8" x 2-3/8" E, from each of the four different fabrics. Sub-cut in half diagonally once. Yield: 4 triangles from each fabric.
2. Cut 4 pieces 2" x 2", A2, from each of the four different fabrics. Yield: 16

Star centers: 1 fabric required

1. Cut 5 pieces C 3-1/2" x 3-1/2"

Assembly:

1. Make 8 double half-square triangles using 8 background B1 (2" x 3-1/2") and all the A2 (2" x 2") star point pieces - 16 total. Refer to the General Instructions for "Making double half-square triangles". ***NOTE:*** Make 2 double half-square triangles from each of the four fabric selections.
2. Before assembling the DE sections, the entire block must be laid out to ensure correct fabric placement. Follow Diagram 1 for layout.
3. Sew respective triangles E to pieces D. See Diagram 2. Press seams away from center.
4. Add opposite triangles and press seam away from center. This block should measure 3-1/2" x 3-1/2". See Diagram 2.
5. Layout and assembly for center star unit: See Diagram 3.

Accent strip around center unit:

1. Cut 2 strips 3/4" wide of accent fabric. Sub-cut into 2 strips 3/4" x 12-1/2" and 2 strips 3/4" x 13".
2. Sew the 12-1/2" strips to opposite sides of the star unit. Press seam away from center. Sew the 13" strips to the right and left sides of the unit. Press out.

Adding Sections F:

1. Cut 2 squares 8-3/4" x 8-3/4". Sub-cut (see General Instructions for sub-cutting) these squares in half diagonally once.
2. Cut 2 strips 1-1/8" wide from a dark border fabric (which will be used 3 times). Sew one short side of each triangle to the strip. See Diagram 4.
3. Press dark strip away from triangles. With a template ruler and rotary cutter, trim way the excess fabric strip by lining up the ruler with

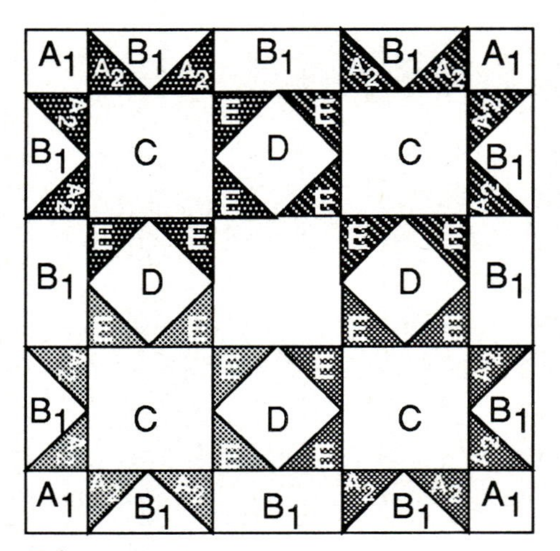

Diagram 1.

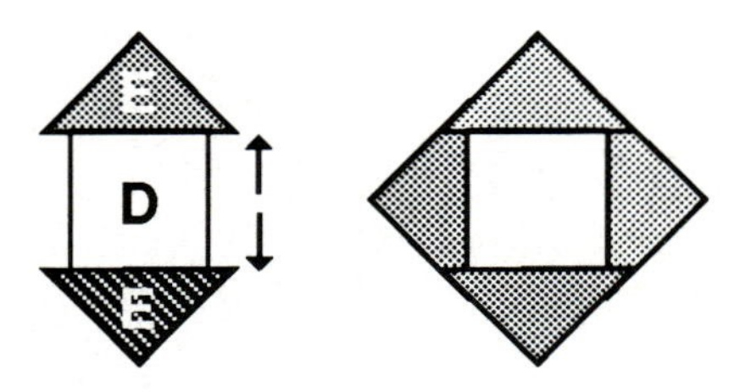

Diagram 2.

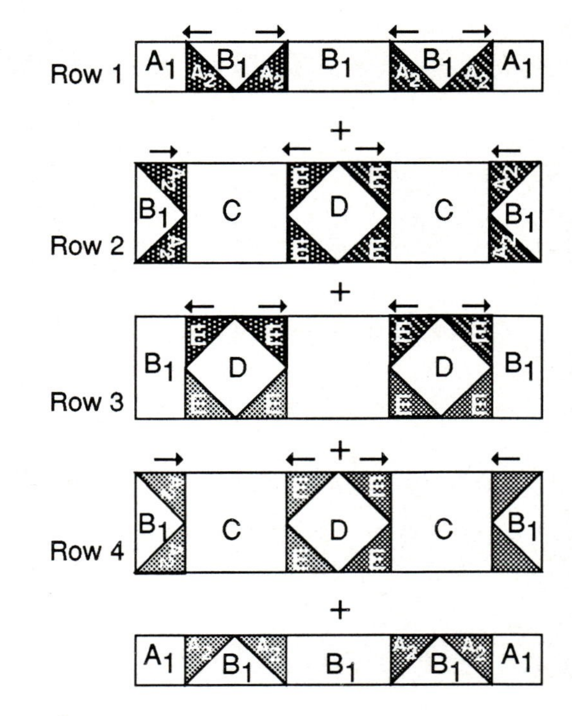

Diagram 3.

—Join the blocks in each row together.

—Press seams in direction of the arrows.

—Join rows together, carefully butting (see General Instructions for butting seams) seams.

—This unit should measure 12-1/2" x 12-1/2" including seam allowances.

triangle. See Diagram 5.
4. Repeat this procedure when seaming the dark strip to the other short side of the triangle. See Diagram 6.
5. Sew long side of the triangles to the center block. Pin and sew one set of opposite sides first. Press seams away from center block. Sew the two opposite remaining sides on. Press out. This unit should now measure 18-1/2" x 18-1/2" including seam allowances. Refer to whole quilt diagram.

Sawtooth border: 1 light and 1 medium value fabric required.
1. Cut 2 strips 2-3/8" wide from the light fabric. Sub-cut into 24 - 2-3/8" squares G1 and 4 squares 2" x 2", H.
2. Cut 2 strips 2-3/8" wide from medium/dark fabric. Sub-cut into 24 - 2-3/8" squares G2.
3. Refer to "Making half-square triangles" in the General Instructions. Follow directions as stated. "Proof" (see General Instructions) your squares to be 2" x 2". Yield: 48.
4. Join the half square triangles into 4 strip sections. See Diagram 7. Section 1 should measure 18-1/2" long. Section 2 should measure 21-1/2" long.
5. Seam a section 1 to opposite sides of the center star unit. Press seams toward center block.
6. Add the section 2 strips to opposite sides. Press seams toward center. The center unit should now measure 21-1/2" x 21-1/2" including seam allowances.

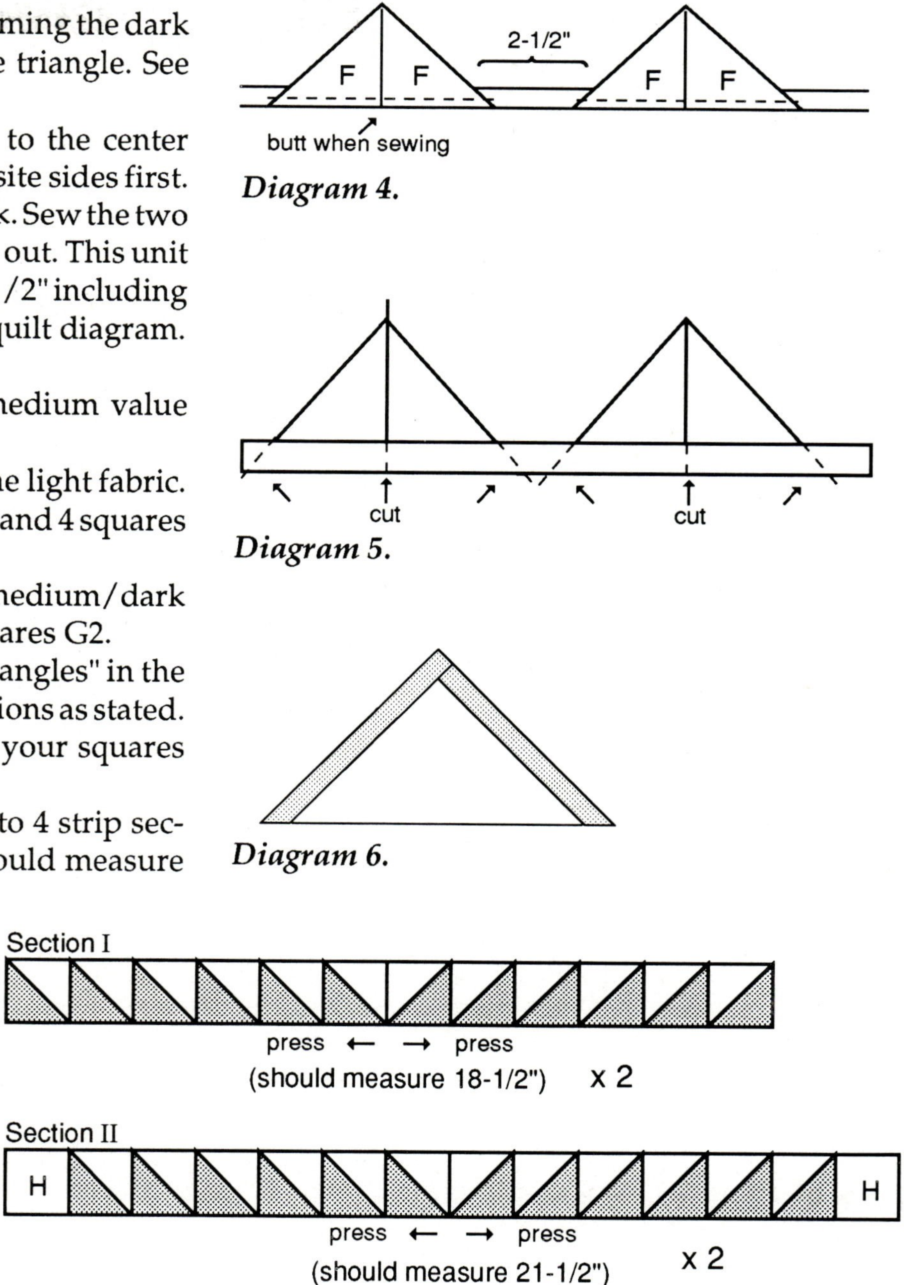

Diagram 4.

Diagram 5.

Diagram 6.

Diagram 7.

Fabric border strip: requires one medium/light fabric
1. Cut 3 strips 2" wide. Cut 2 pieces 21-1/2" from one strip. Cut one 24-1/2" piece from each of the remaining two strips.
2. Seam the two shorter strips to opposite sides. Press seam away from center. Seam top and bottom borders. Center unit should now measure 24-1/2" x 24-1/2".

Windmill border:
For windmills: 5 backgrounds and 5 medium to

medium/dark fabrics are required. For setting fabric around the windmills, 1 medium background is required. For border inset triangles, 1 medium/dark is required. One dark is required for border strip.

Windmill cutting and assembly: a total of 20 windmill blocks are required.
1. From each of the 5 backgrounds cut 8 squares 2-3/8" x 2-3/8".
2. From each of the 5 medium to medium dark fabrics, cut 8 squares 2-3/8" x 2-3/8".
3. Refer to the General Instructions under "Making half-square triangles". Follow directions exactly. *NOTE:* Make sure when pairing up the fabrics, that you have 2 background squares and 2 medium/dark squares the same. You need 4 half-square triangles to make one windmill block. Proof the half-square triangles to 2" x 2".
4. Assemble the windmill blocks: See Diagram 8. Match points and butt seams when sewing blocks together. Press. Assemble 20 windmill blocks. The blocks should be 3-1/2" x 3-1/2".
5. From a medium background, cut 3 strips 3" wide. Sub-cut into 40 3" x 3" squares. Sub-cut these in half diagonally once to yield 80 triangles.
6. Sew a triangle to top and bottom of a windmill block. See Diagram 9. Press seam away from the block. Add triangles J to remaining sides. Press. Complete all 20 windmill blocks in this manner. The blocks should measure 4-3/4" x 4-3/4".

Inset triangles K: trace, cut, and transfer all markings to template K (Template K on page 90).
1. Cut 4 strips 3-5/8" wide from the medium inset fabric.
2. Cut 10 strips 1" wide from dark border strip fabric. Set aside 2 of the strips for later use.
3. Sew an 1" strip to either side of a 3-5/8" wide strip, previously cut in #1. Press seams away from the center. Repeat for all 4 strip sections.
4. Lay template K on the strip sets and trace and cut. You can cut approximately 9 template K's from each strip set. You need a total of 32 K pieces. See Diagram 10.

Corners R: 8 corners required
1. Cut 4 squares 3-5/8" x 3-5/8" from same fabric

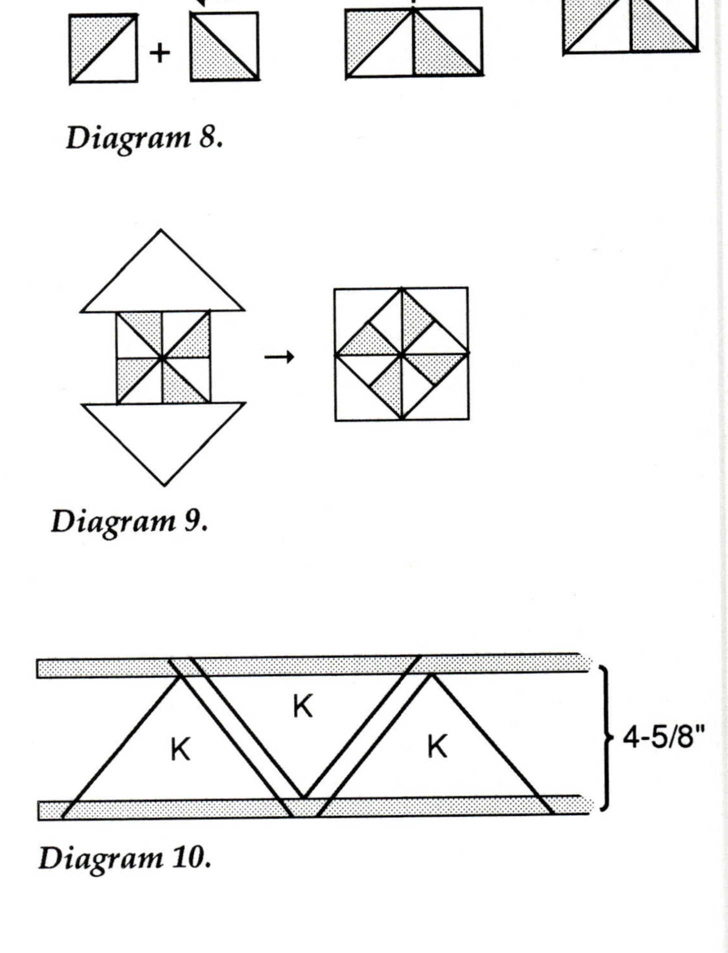

Diagram 8.

Diagram 9.

Diagram 10.

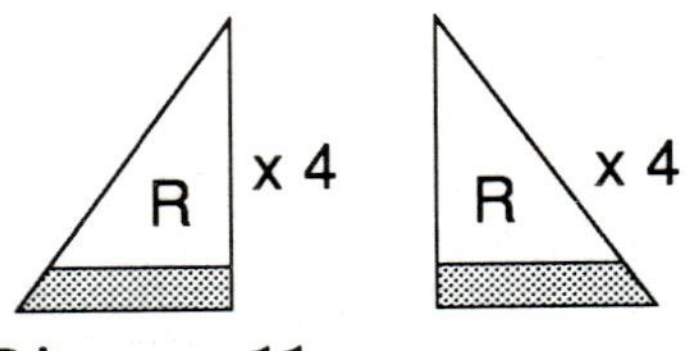

Diagram 11.

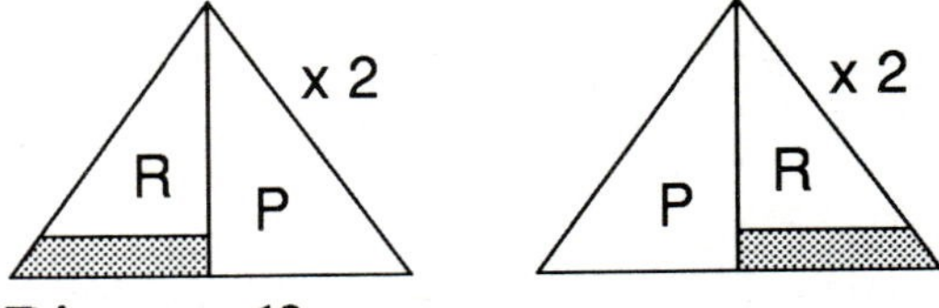

Diagram 12.

Medallion: 45" x 45"

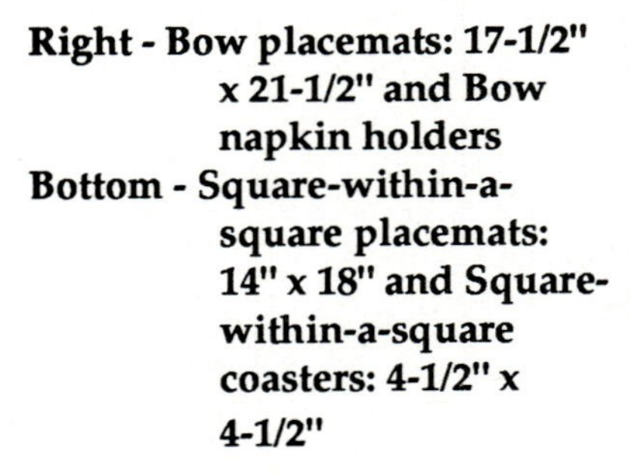

Right - Bow placemats: 17-1/2" x 21-1/2" and Bow napkin holders
Bottom - Square-within-a-square placemats: 14" x 18" and Square-within-a-square coasters: 4-1/2" x 4-1/2"

Judy's table runner: 14-1/2" x 44-1/2"

Above - Star Placemats: 14" x 18", Star coasters: 4-1/2" x 4-1/2", and Spice mats: 9" x 9"
Right - Gift wrap, Primitive mitten ornaments, Raggedy Santa ornaments, and Nature's garland

Above - Judy's table runner in Christmas fabrics: 14"-1/2" x 44-1/2"
Right - Log cabin heart ornaments (or pin cushions), and Nature's garland

Above - **Windmill pillow: 10" x 10", Log cabin pillow: 11" x 11", Charn dash pillow: 11-1/2" x 11-1/2"**

Right - **Charn dash mini quilt: 17" x 17" and Windmill mini quilt: 15-1/2" x 15-1/2"**

Scrappy stars quilt: 72" x 93-1/2"

Victorian tree: Nosegays, Victorian heart ornaments, Victorian mitten ornaments, Glass ball ornaments, Gift baskets, and gift wrap

Above - Gift wrap, Quilter's gift basket, Victorian heart ornament, Cook's gift basket, and Glass ball ornaments
Left - Glass ball ornaments

Above - Framed mini quilts - Sunburst: (framed size) 14-1/4" x 14-1/4", Cake stand: (framed size) 10-1/4" x 8-1/2", and Shoo fly: (framed size) 8-1/2" x 8-1/2"

Left - Victorian heart ornament (pincushion), Nosegay, Victorian mitten ornament, Quilter's gift basket, and Heart sachet (in basket)

Mini sampler quilt: 15" x 19"

Mini medallion quilt: 17" x 21"

Zig-zag quilt: 29" x 36"

Raggedy Santa ornaments, Nature's garland, Log cabin heart ornaments, Log cabin pillow, Scrappy star pillow, Gift wrap, and Men's gift basket

Above - Log cabin pillow: 11" x 11", Scrappy star pillow: 15" x 15", and Men's gift basket
Right - Gift wrap, Men's gift basket, and Quilter's gift basket

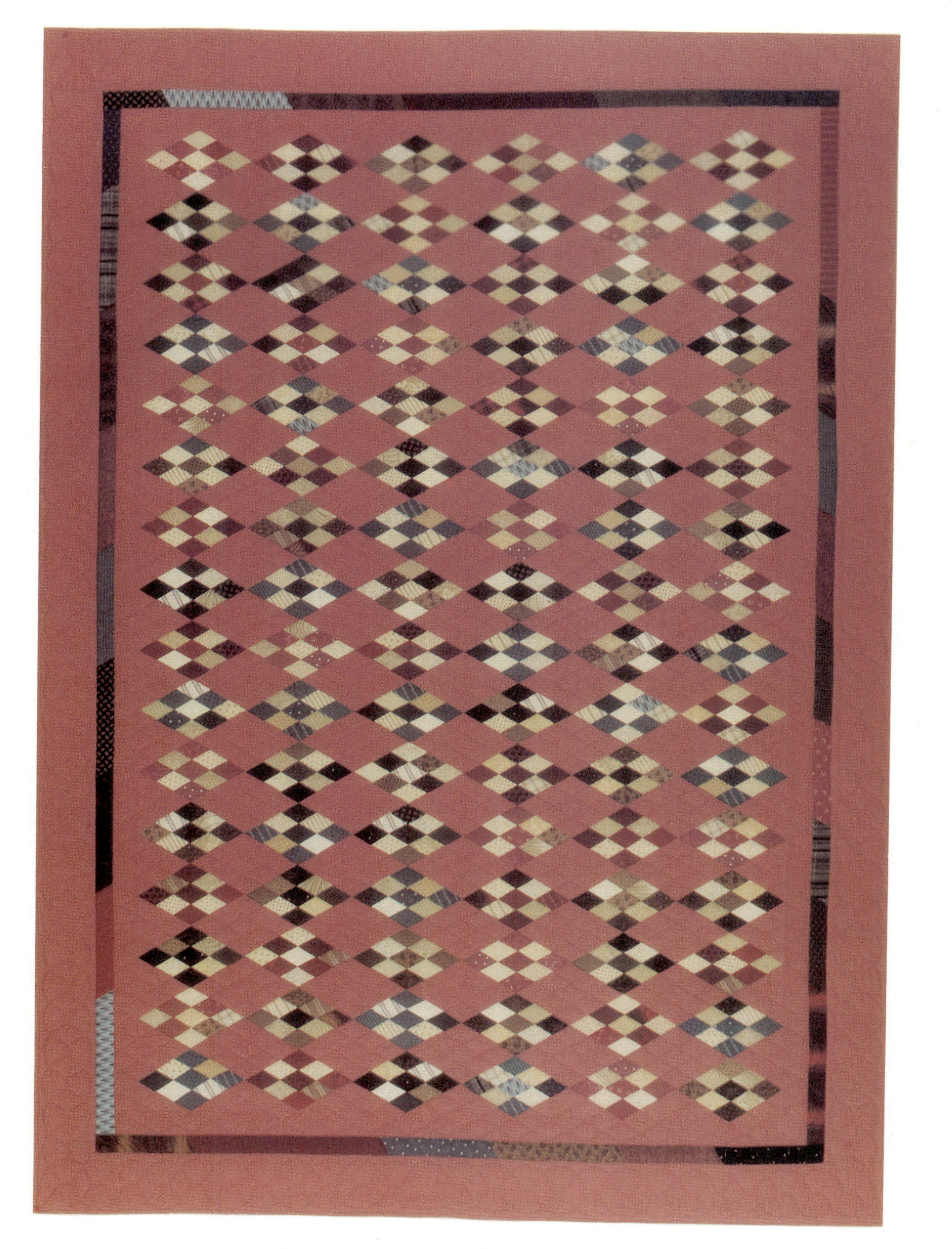

Diagonal nine-patch quilt: 68" x 96"

Country cross-roads quilt: 87-1/2" x 105"

as used for K above. Sub-cut in half diagonally once.

2. Sew 4 triangles to 1" wide strip (previously cut in step #2 under Inset triangles K) along one short edge of each triangle. (Refer back to Diagram 4). Sew the 4 remaining triangles to the 1" wide strip in mirror image of the first four. See Diagram 11.

3. Press seam away from strip. Trim excess fabric from triangle edges as previously done.

4. For triangles P: Cut 2 squares 4-1/4" x 4-1/4" from same medium fabric as for K. Sub-cut in half diagonally once to yield 4 P.

5. Join 4 P to 4 R as shown in Diagram 12. Set aside.

Outer border corners O: 4 required

1. Cut 2 squares 3-5/8" x 3-5/8". Sub-cut in half diagonally once to yield 4 pieces O.

2. Retrieve the remaining 1" border strip. Sew a short triangle side to strip as previously done. Press. Trim excess away. Sew remaining short triangle edge to the remainder of the 1" strip as previously done in Diagram 6.

Assembling side borders:

1. Lay out the side borders according to Diagram 13.

2. Lay out the top and bottom borders. Proceed to sew after studying Diagram 14. Sew two border strips in this fashion.

3. Assemble the four corner units. See Diagram 15.

Attaching the borders to the center star unit:

1. Pin and sew side borders to center unit according to Diagram 16. Press.

2. Pin and sew top and bottom borders to center unit according to Diagram 16. Press.

3. Pin and sew corner sections to center unit according to Diagram 16 on the following page. Press.

Plain fabric border:

1. Cut 4 strips 1-1/2" wide.

2. Follow the instructions for "Bordering a quilt" in the General Instructions.

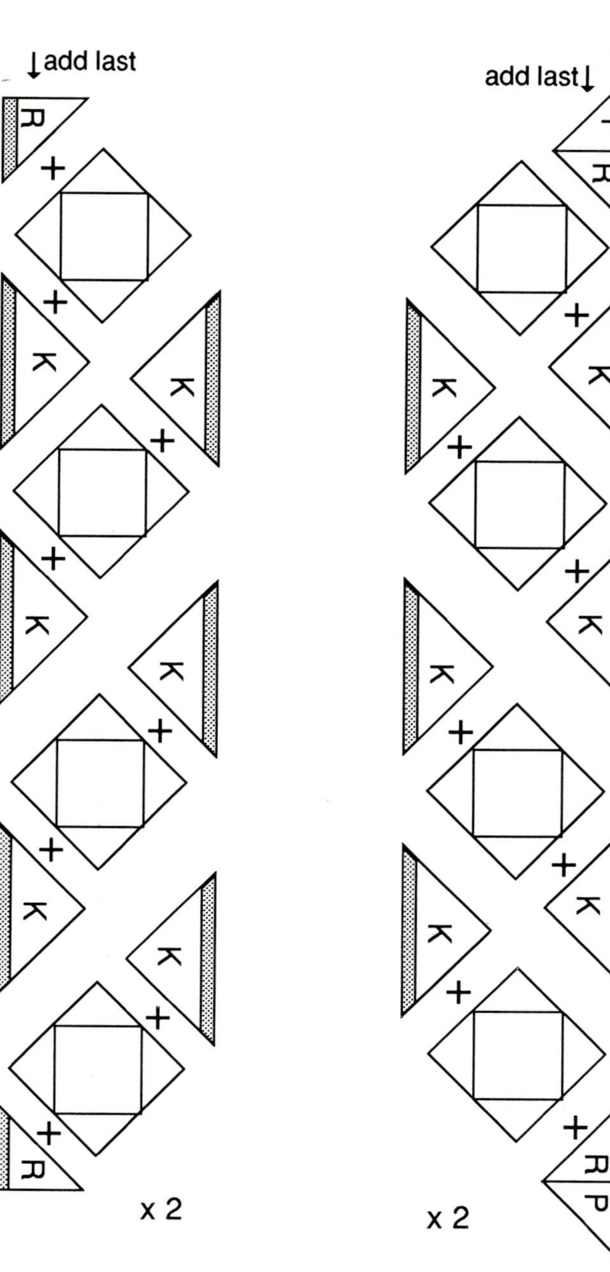

Diagram 13. *Diagram 14.*

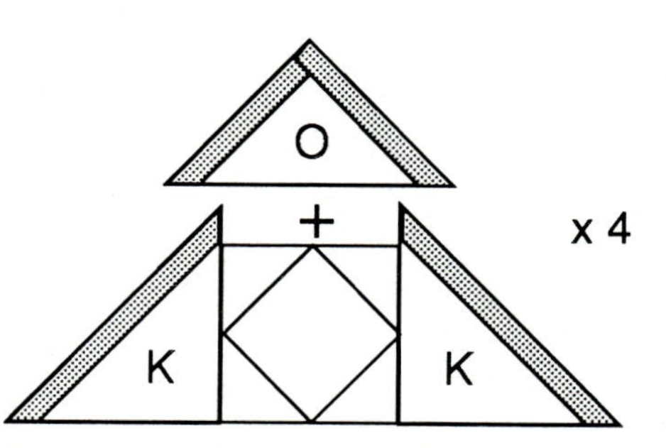

Diagram 15.

Final border: one dark fabric required
1. Cut 4 strips 3-1/2" wide.
2. Follow the instructions for "Bordering a quilt" in the General Instructions. ***NOTE:*** You may have to piece the top and bottom borders if your fabric isn't wide enough.

Finishing the quilt:
1. Decide on the desired quilting design. Mark the quilt top accordingly.
2. Cut a piece of batting and backing to fit the quilt top. The backing will have to be pieced.
3. Cut 5 strips of binding 2-1/4" wide.
4. Follow the General Instructions for layering up a quilt, hand or machine quilting, and binding.

Diagram 16.

Log Cabin Heart Ornaments

Fabric and supply requirements:
— Scraps of light and dark fabrics for "Logs"
— 2-1/2" square of a dark fabric for "center"
— 5" square each of muslin and backing fabric
— Small amount of polyester fiberfil stuffing
— Small piece of twine or 1/16" wide ribbon for hanger

Instructions:
1. Trace and cut the heart pattern from template plastic. Transfer all markings.
2. Cut one 5" square of muslin, one 5" square of backing fabric, and one 2-1/2" square of dark print for "center".
3. Cut various light and dark 1" wide strips for the "logs". Cut 4 lights and 4 darks.
4. Draw a diagonal line on muslin base. Place 2-1/2" square in corner of block with point lining up with diagonal line. Lay a light strip of fabric, right sides together, on the righthand side of fabric square. Stitch 1/4" seam to end of square. See Diagram 2. Trim excess even with square. Finger press strip open. Lay a dark strip on left side of square, right sides together, and seam 1/4" to the end of light fabric strip. Trim excess. Finger press. The corner of the second strip when pressed open should hit on the diagonal line drawn on muslin square. Every other strip sewn should hit on this line. Continue sewing alternating a light fabric with a darker fabric until you have sewn four strips on either side. Press. See Diagram 3.
5. Turn stripped piece over. Draw a diagonal line on the wrong side, the line will intersect the stitching lines. Place the heart pattern on the back of muslin, lining up the diagonal line on the pattern with the drawn line. Make sure there is a 1/4" extra for seam allowance on all sides of the heart pattern. Trace heart onto muslin.
6. Place right sides together of pieced heart and backing square. Don't cut out heart yet. Stitch on traced line leaving about 2" open on side. Clip the place where the two curves meet. Turn right side out. Stuff lightly. Slip-stitch closed.

Diagram 1.

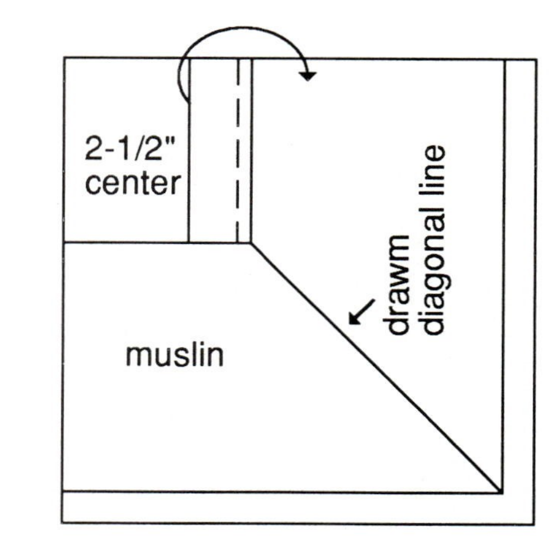

Diagram 2.

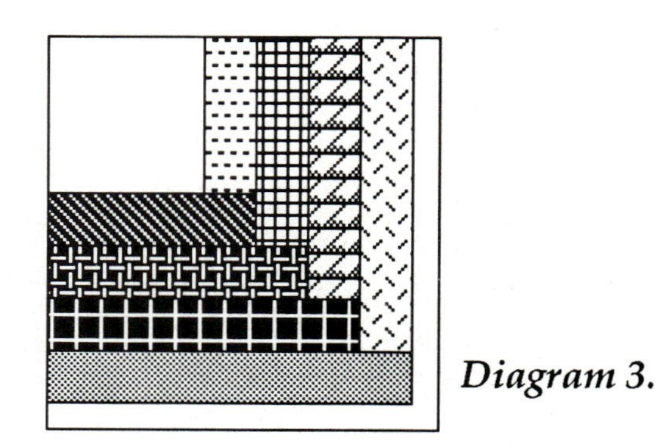

Diagram 3.

7. Thread either lightweight twine or 1/16" ribbon onto a large eyed needle. Attach a "hanger" by inserting the needle through both thicknesses of heart where the curves of the heart meet. Make a 3" loop. Tie a knot.

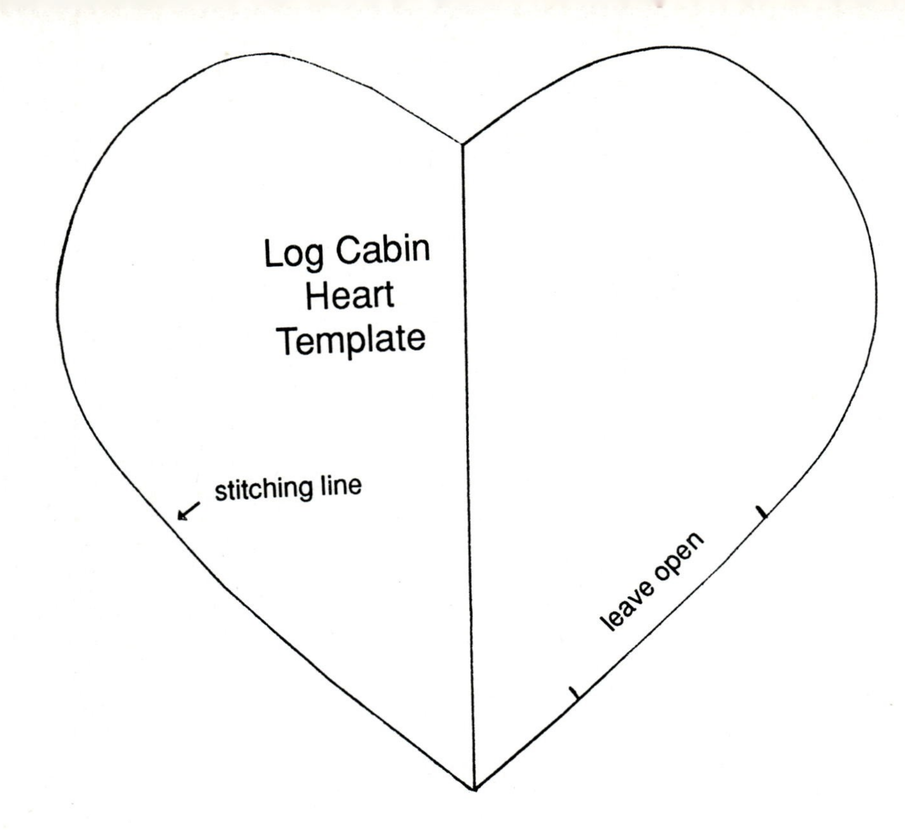

Nature's Garland

If stored in an airtight container, this garland may last for years. It will be a totally "natural" addition to your Christmas tree or mantel.

Supplies:
—Dried apple slices: 2 cups lemon juice, 3 tbls. salt
—Nuts and acorns
—Cinnamon sticks
—Bay leaves
—Dried cranberries
—Large eyed needle
—Medium weight fishing tackle line
—Drill and an 1/16" drill bit
—Clear acrylic spray

Instructions for making dried apple slices:
1. For dried apple slices, cut approximately 1/4" wide slices from small round apples. (Discard the end pieces).
2. Soak the apple slices (completely covered) in a mixture of lemon juice and salt: 2 cups of lemon juice and 3 tablespoons of salt. Soak the slices for about 15 minutes.
3. Blot excess lemon juice from apple slices with paper towels.
4. Place the slices (single layer) on wire cooling racks. Bake at 150° for approximately 5-6 hours. Turn the slices over every hour so they dry evenly and don't curl up. The slices are dry when they have a leathery feel.
5. Place apple slices, single layer, on newspaper. Spray two light coats of clear acrylic spray on them. Turn apple slices over and repeat.

Instructions for nuts and acorns:
1. Select nuts that have no cracks in them.
2. Drill a small hole through the nuts.

Instructions for cinnamon sticks:

1. Try to buy the cinnamon sticks from a bulk food warehouse or craft store.
2. Sticks between 1-1/2" to 3" work best.
3. Save leftover broken sticks for use in a pot-pourri.

Bay leaves:

Once again, try to buy the bay leaves in bulk from a health food store or a bulk food ware-house. They are much too expensive to buy in individual cans for the amount needed here.

Dried cranberries:

Let the cranberries dry in an open basket for a couple of weeks before you are ready to use them.

Garland assembly:

1. Thread an end of the tackle line onto needle. Don't cut the piece off yet.
2. Thread about 3 cinnamon sticks onto the line.
3. Thread about 10 bay leaves on next.
4. Thread assorted nuts and the cranberries on intermittently with the bay leaves, dried applies, and cinnamon sticks. There is no absolute order for threading these items on.
5. Tie off the line when the garland reaches 4-5 feet long. Tie off the line by repeatedly going through the last nut hole, looping a knot each time.
6. Place garland on newspaper. Lightly spray acrylic spray on both sides of garland to further preserve it.
7. Store in a dry place.

Raggedy Santa Ornament

Fabric and supply requirements:
— Scraps of tea-dyed muslin
— 2 - 3-1/2" x 6-1/2" pieces of muslin
— Scraps of red print fabric for hat
—Small amount of polyester batting
—Red crayon and black permanent marking pen
—Scrap of tea-dyed Pellon fleece or batting (Cut the required piece of batting then spray it with some strong tea). Cotton batting works best (1/2" x 6").
— Small jingle bell for hat (optional)
— 6" piece of twine or string for hanger
— Large eyed needle

Trace and cut from template plastic the templates for Santa head and hat. Transfer all markings onto your template.

Instructions for ornament:
1. Trace (do not cut yet) the Santa head onto tea-dyed muslin. Through double thickness of muslin, stitch on the drawn line, leaving the bottom open according to the template pattern. Cut 1/8" - 1/4" around the stitching line.
2. Lay two pieces of hat fabric right sides together. Trace hat template onto fabric. Stitch on the drawn line leaving the bottom open. Cut out 1/8" - 1/4" around stitching line. Turn right side out.
3. Turn the head right side out. Stuff with fiberfill. Stitch bottom closed.
4. Cut 2 pieces 3-1/2" x 6-1/2" from muslin for the beard.
5. With beard pieces layered, make cuts every 1/2", about 1" deep. See Diagram 1.
6. Carefully tear the strips up to 1/2" from the top of piece.
7. Sew (by hand) a running stitch (through both layers) across the top of the beard about 1/4" from the top edge. Pull this thread to gather beard to approximately 2-1/2" wide. Knot thread off. See Diagram 1.
8. Place beard on Santa face, referring to markings on the pattern template. Either stitch or hot glue the beard in place. Trim beard, rounding side edges.
9. Hot glue hat to head, referring to placement lines on pattern. Hot glue a 1/2" x 6" wide piece of tea-dyed batting around bottom of hat. Flop hat down and hot glue jingle bell in place.
10. Give Santa some rosy cheeks with a red crayon or blush. Mark eyes with permanent marking pen. * * See pattern for placement.
11. Thread hanger (twine or string) through large eyed needle. Attach the hanger at the top of hat.

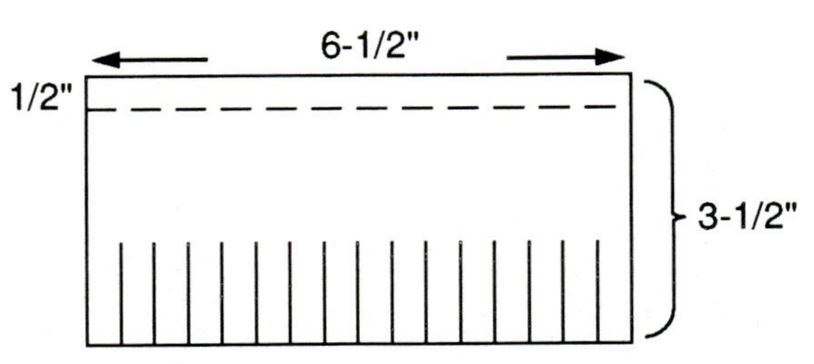

Diagram 1.

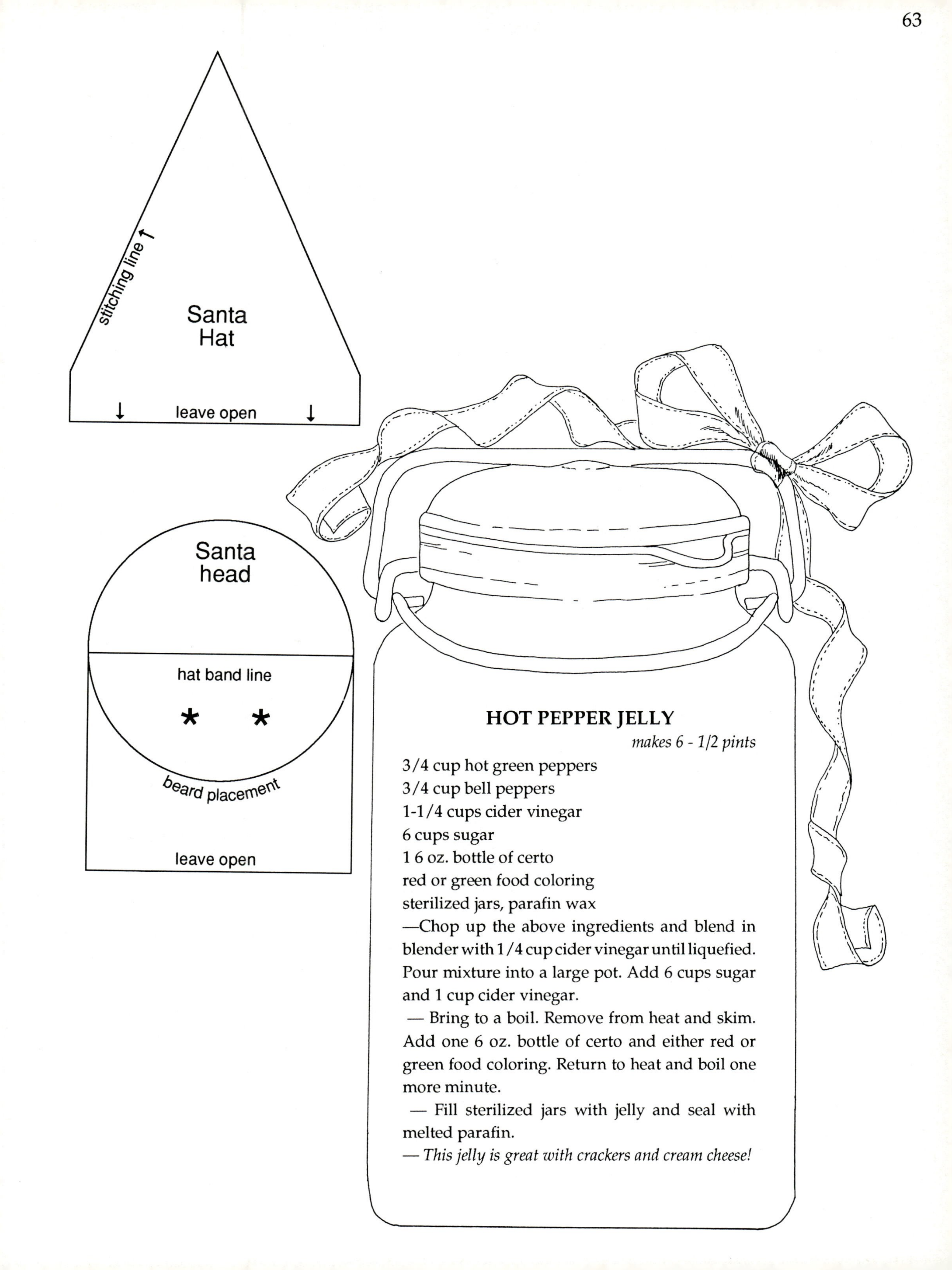

HOT PEPPER JELLY

makes 6 - 1/2 pints

3/4 cup hot green peppers
3/4 cup bell peppers
1-1/4 cups cider vinegar
6 cups sugar
1 6 oz. bottle of certo
red or green food coloring
sterilized jars, parafin wax

—Chop up the above ingredients and blend in blender with 1/4 cup cider vinegar until liquefied. Pour mixture into a large pot. Add 6 cups sugar and 1 cup cider vinegar.

— Bring to a boil. Remove from heat and skim. Add one 6 oz. bottle of certo and either red or green food coloring. Return to heat and boil one more minute.

— Fill sterilized jars with jelly and seal with melted parafin.

— This jelly is great with crackers and cream cheese!

Primitive Mitten Ornaments

Fabric and supply requirements:
— Scraps of an old unsalvagable quilt or newly made patchwork made to look old. (Instructions for making "old looking" patchwork may be found below.)
— 8" piece of twine
— 5" x 10" piece of backing fabric for one pair of mittens.

Instructions for making "old looking patchwork":
1. Gather up all your unfinished projects or unused single blocks. (I'm sure you have a few!) Piece a few blocks together with various sized strips of fabric.
2. Layer up this piece (I work with pieces that are approximately 10" x 20") according to "Layering up a quilt" in the General Instructions. In order to achieve the "old" look, try to use 100% cotton batting.
3. Machine quilt stitch-in-a ditch fashion, or randomly on your block section.
4. Wash the quilted piece in the washing machine with warm water. Toss in the dryer to dry. Your piece should now have a puffy, worn look. Now proceed to make those cute mittens!
Instructions for making mittens:
1. Trace and cut out mitten pattern from template plastic. Transfer all markings to plastic pattern. (Template on following page.)
2. Trace mittens on wrong side of quilted fabric, making sure you allow for the 1/4" seam allowance. Cut the fabric in rectangular pieces around traced mittens. Place rectangles right sides together, on the backing fabric. Before cutting out, stitch on traced line, leaving the bottom and side of thumb open. Trim seam down to 1/4" when cutting out.
3. Open edge on thumb side of mitten and insert an 8" piece of ribbon or twine through the inside of mitten. Make sure a little tail of ribbon sticks out beyond the seam so it doesn't fray or ravel when sewn. Attach the other end of ribbon or twine to another mitten in the same manner. Sew side seam closed.
4. Clip corner where thumb and hand meet. Turn right side out. Turn under hem at the bottom 1/4" and hem using a running stitch. Hang mittens over a branch on the tree or tie them into the bow on a present.

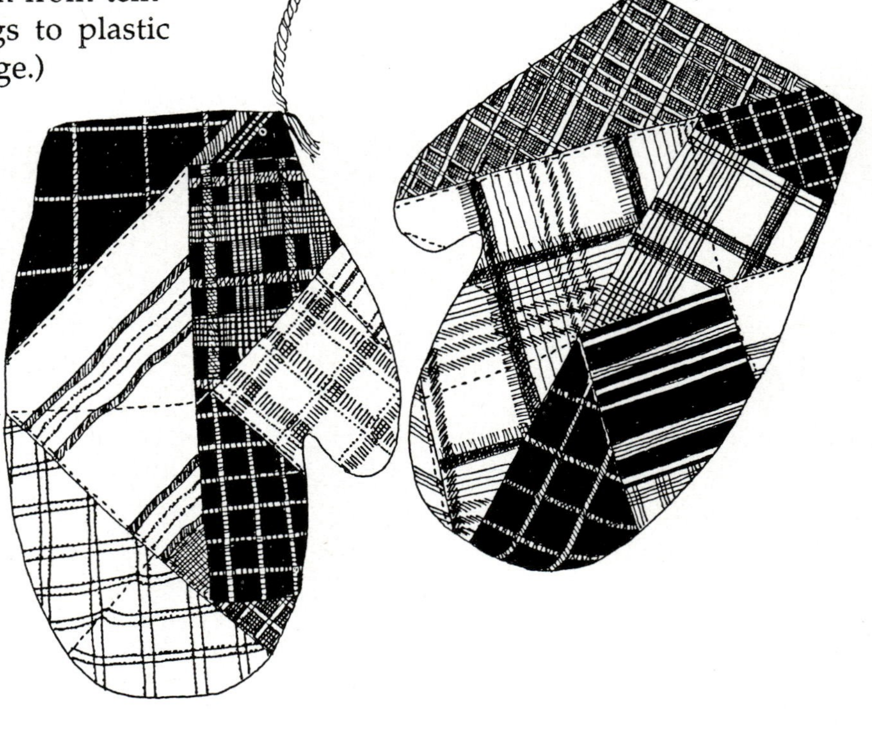

Victorian Mitten Ornaments

Fabric and supply requirements:
— Scraps of brocade, chintz, velvet, or any decorative "Victorian looking" fabric
— 8" piece of 1/16" wide double-faced ribbon
— Scraps of lace and ribbon
— Pre-packaged ribbon rosettes

Instructions for making mittens:
1. Follow the instructions for making mittens under "Primitive Mittens".
2. The front and back sides of these mittens are made of the same fabric.
3. Embellish the tops of the mittens with lace trim, ribbon, and ribbon rosettes.

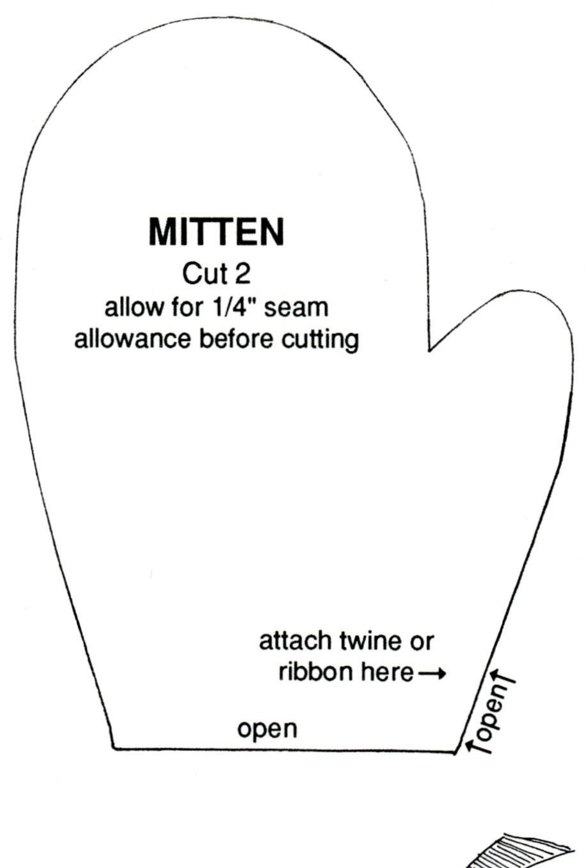

Decorated Glass Ball Ornaments

Supplies:
— Plain glass ball ornaments
—dried flowers such as baby's breath, status, tiny roses, and various colored dried flowers
— Ribbon rosettes
—Sprigs of artificial garland
— Scraps of metallic and satin ribbon
— Decorative metallic braids and trims
— "Cool" hot glue gun

Instructions:
1. Place a dot of hot glue at the top of the glass ball. Wrap the braid or trim around the ball. Glue in place. Wrap another strip of braid or trim around the ball and glue in place. (See colored photo).
2. Cut short pieces of garland and glue around the top of ball.
3. Fill in with baby's breath and other dried flowers. Glue the rosettes or dried roses last.
4. Cut 6" pieces of ribbon for hangers.

Nosegay or Tussie-Mussie

In the nineteenth century, tussie-mussies were given as tokens of affection and love. Each tussie-mussie, or nosegay, was comprised of flowers that actually had special meaning. You could send a message to a person via the type of flowers you had chosen for your tussie-mussie. For instance, a rose means love, a daisy means innocence, and a pansy means thinking of you. For more information on the meaning of flowers, consult an old flower language book or buy a new one. Many herb books would also have this information.

Tussie-mussies make great small gifts, special package decorations, and wonderful shower favors as well as great Christmas tree decorations.

Supply requirements:
—6" white paper doily
—Tape (transparent), and floral tape, 1/4" wide, self-adhesive
—An assortment of greens: bay leaves, dried leaves, eucalyptus leaves and silk leaves, if natural ones are unavailable.
—Dried herbs, roses, and flower heads
—Hot glue gun
—Optional 1/2 yard of 1/4" wide double-faced satin ribbon.

Instructions:
1. Fold doily in half, then in half again. Clip a small hole at the point of doily.
2. Carefully bunch up the doily for a "gathered" effect.
3. Put a couple of sprigs of greens (ones with 3" stems) through the hole. Once again, carefully gather the doily. Tape (transparent) around the base of the doily tightly to ensure a gathered look. (Don't be discouraged, this is the hardest part!) With floral tape, wrap the base of the doily (over the tape) and continue down the stem, overlapping the floral tape slightly.
4. Place the nosegay in a glass or jar so that it is held upright.
5. Now fill in the greens, placing a small amount of hot glue on the ends of stems. Add baby's breath or any herbal "filler". Lastly, glue in a rose (very traditional to a nosegay) and other flower heads.
6. Wrap the ribbon twice around the base of the nosegay and tie a bow.

Victorian Heart Ornament or Pin Cushion

Diagram 1.

Fabric and supply requirements:

—5" square of muslin
—Scraps of chintz, brocade, satin, velvet, polished cotton, water taffeta, and a 5" square of one of these fabrics for the heart backing
—1/2 yard pre-gathered 1" wide lace
—Assorted double-faced ribbons (I like using 3/8" wide ribbon for tails along with 1/8" wide ribbon for the hanger and bow)
—Assorted perle cotton or embroidery floss
—Assorted beads
—Metallic embroidery thread
—Optional fancy braided trims (scraps)
—Small amount of polyester fiberfil
—Optional small amount of potpourri
—Template plastic

Instructions:

1. Trace, cut out, and transfer all markings onto the heart template.
2. Center and trace the heart onto 5" square of muslin. Turn muslin square over. Place it on a window, TV, or light box. Retrace the outline of the heart onto this side of the muslin. The traced line is your guideline for stitching. All sewn pieces of fabric must extend at least 1/4" past the drawn line.
3. Choose three fabric scraps that go well together. Trim up the scraps so that you have at least one straight edge.
4. Place scraps on muslin base right side up. Place another scrap, straight edge even with first strip, and right sides together, onto first piece.
5. Stitch 1/4" seam. Open piece out. Finger press. Add a third scrap of fabric in same manner. I have given you some examples to get you started. See Diagram 1. Just remember not to trim to the drawn line — that is your seamline.
6. Turn the pieced heart over. Using the traced heart on the back as your guide, trim to 1/4" from stitching line.
7. Now refer to the "Embroidery stitching chart". Embellish the heart with stitches on all seamlines. Add trims and beads. Embellish any areas of the heart that is "plain". Try not to extend the beading into the seamline. Securely knot off all work.
8. Pin pre-gathered lace to edge of heart, right sides together. Start pinning on a side of the heart, leaving about 1/2" extra lace at the beginning and end. Now make a seam on the lace where the two end pieces of lace meet. Trim seam to 1/8".
9. Stitch lace to heart using 1/4" seam.

10. Place the backing square on top of pieced heart, right sides together. Pin. Stitch pieces together following the previous stitching line. Remember to leave a 2" opening on one side of the heart.
11. Turn right sides out. Stuff lightly with polyfil. (You may want to add some potpourri before stitching the heart closed). Slip stitch the opening closed.
12. Cut 9" of ribbon for the hanger. Fold in half and pin on heart front, leaving ends hanging a bit. Tie a bow with coordinating or the same ribbon. Place it on top of the hanger ribbon. Tack both hanger and bow in place with a few stitches.

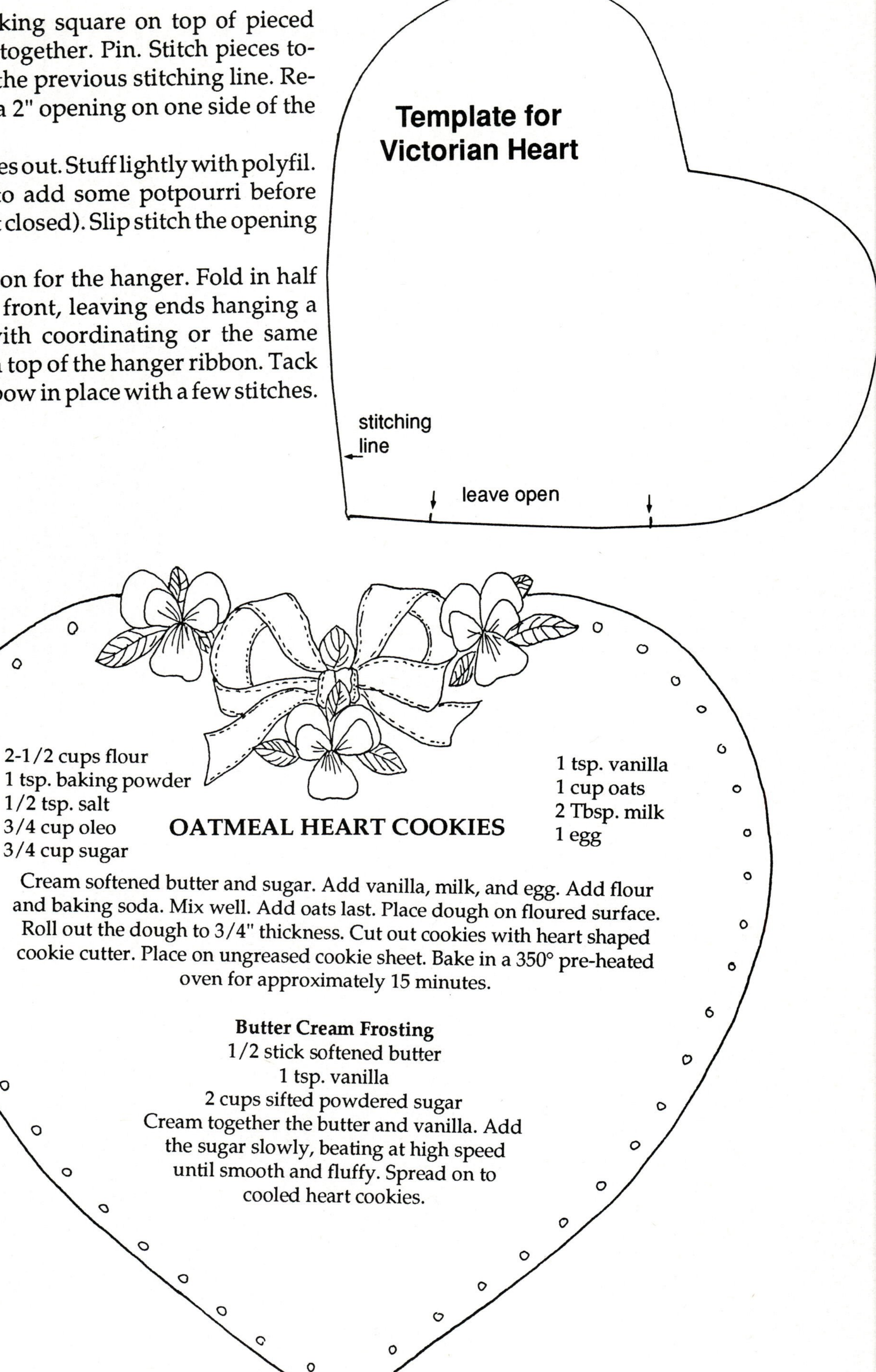

OATMEAL HEART COOKIES

2-1/2 cups flour
1 tsp. baking powder
1/2 tsp. salt
3/4 cup oleo
3/4 cup sugar
1 tsp. vanilla
1 cup oats
2 Tbsp. milk
1 egg

Cream softened butter and sugar. Add vanilla, milk, and egg. Add flour and baking soda. Mix well. Add oats last. Place dough on floured surface. Roll out the dough to 3/4" thickness. Cut out cookies with heart shaped cookie cutter. Place on ungreased cookie sheet. Bake in a 350° pre-heated oven for approximately 15 minutes.

Butter Cream Frosting
1/2 stick softened butter
1 tsp. vanilla
2 cups sifted powdered sugar
Cream together the butter and vanilla. Add the sugar slowly, beating at high speed until smooth and fluffy. Spread on to cooled heart cookies.

EMBROIDERY CHART

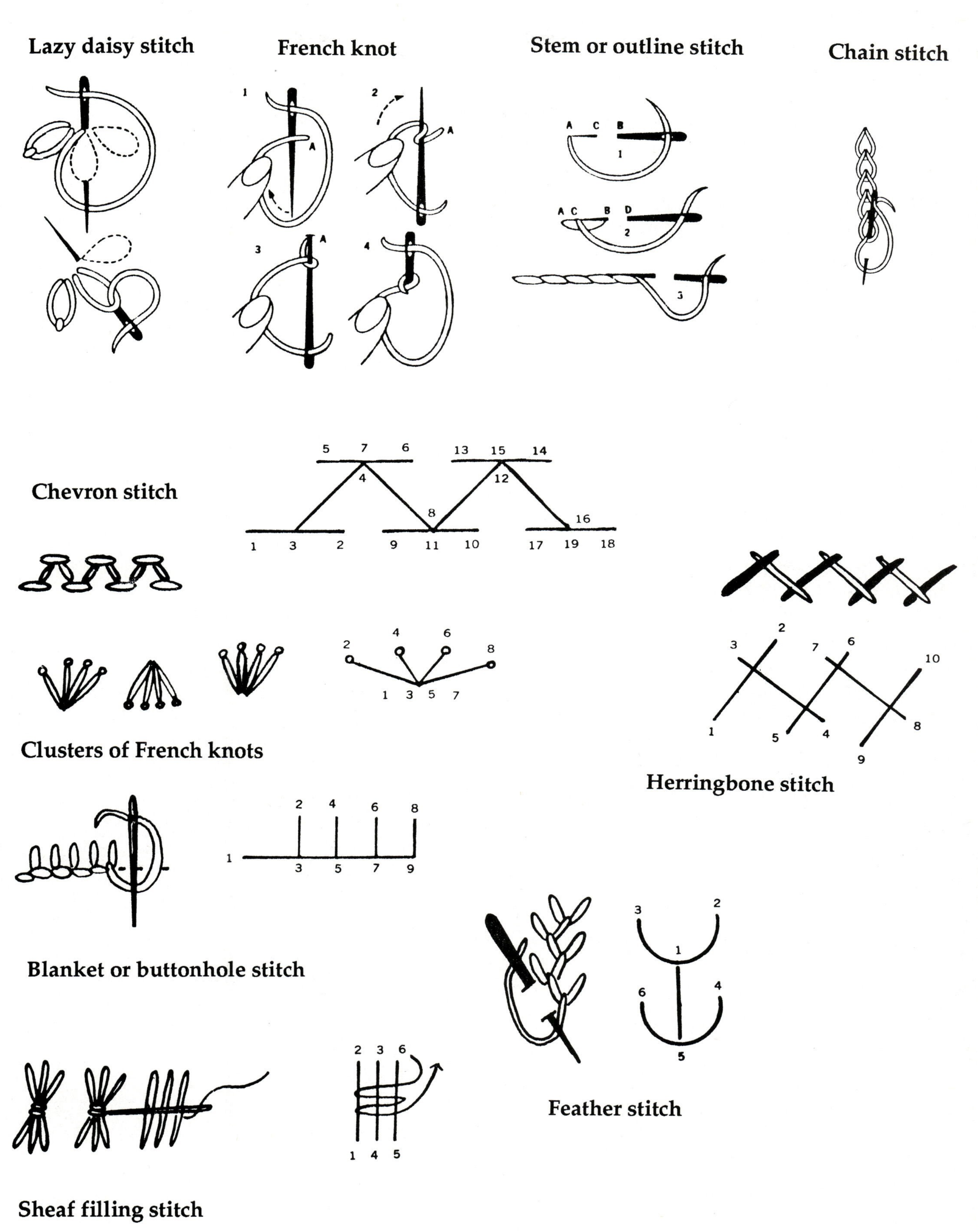

Heart Sachets

These little heart sachets are great for tucking in drawers, suitcases, sheets and towels. They are easy to make and fun to give! They also make great shower party favors.

Fabric and supply requirements:
—2 - 5" x 5" squares of floral fabric
—Scraps of ribbon
—Glue (hot glue gun works best)
—4 teaspoons of potpourri
—Pinking shears
—Template plastic

Instructions:
1. Trace, cut out, and transfer all markings to plastic heart template.
2. Trace heart template on to right side of one square of floral fabric. Place squares of fabric *wrong* sides together, with traced heart facing up. Stitch through both thicknesses on the drawn line, leaving a 2" opening on one side of the heart.
3. Pink around the edges of the heart about 1/4" from the edge of drawn line.
4. Place potpourri in heart.
5. Top stitch opening closed.
6. Tie a bow and glue it to the top of heart where the two curves meet.

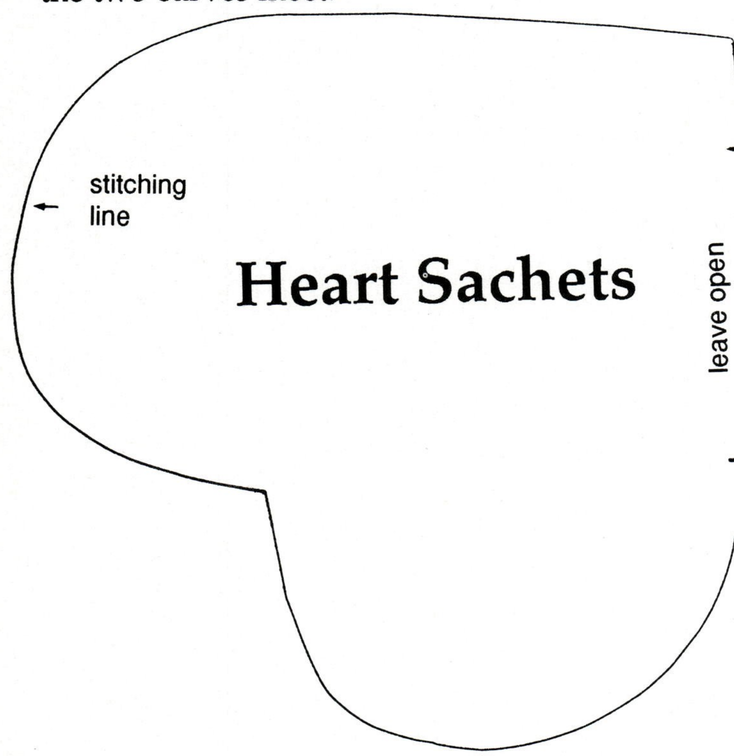

Spicy Heart Mug Mat

Everytime you set your hot mug of coffee or tea on this mat, a spicy aroma fills the air.

Fabric and supply requirements:
Refer to heart sachets for heart template and all requirements.
NOTE: Change the 4 teaspoons of herbal potpourri to 4 teaspoons of crushed cinnamon sticks and whole cloves.
Instructions:
Refer to heart sachets for all instructions.

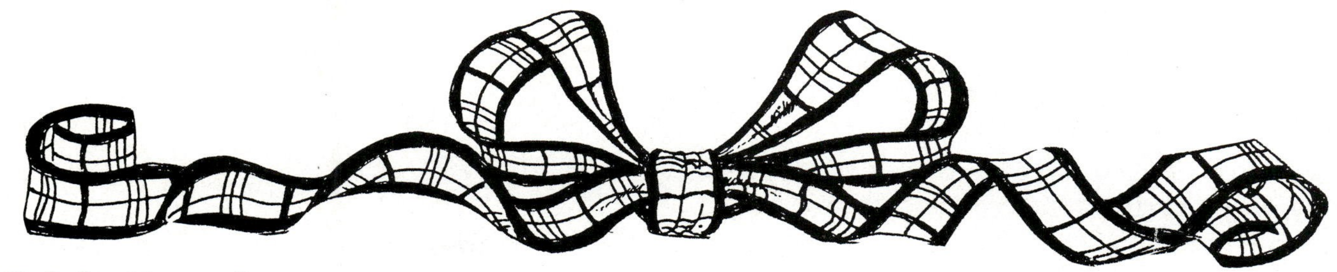

Gift Baskets

Giving a gift basket is a very personal way of showing someone that you care. Take a minute to think about the receiver's personal interests and pastimes, or build your gift basket idea around an important event. The theme for your gift basket will suggest many ideas.

I find that herbs, herbal teas, and potpourris seem to always be included in my gift baskets. I have included a list of herbal teas and herbal bath sachets which are wonderful additions to any gift basket. Perhaps you may even want to attach a tag to the tea or bath sachet explaining its contents and "remedies".

The following ideas are a few gift basket suggestions just to get you started:

For the quilter:

Include a heart pin cushion (instructions on page 67), bundles of fabric tied up with ribbon, quilting needles, retractable tape measure, spice mug mat (instructions on page 70), herbal tea and mug, jar of cherry jam (recipe on page 11), and a loaf of cherry nut bread (recipe on page 88).

For the cook:

Include recipe cards, heart-shaped cookie cutters, decorative tin filled with oatmeal heart cookies (recipe on page 68), recipe for oatmeal heart cookies, spice mat (instructions on page 70), mug, small bag of instant cocoa with attached recipe (recipe on page 9), jar of cherry jam (recipe on page 11), and a raggedy Santa ornament (instructions on page 62).

For the graduate:

Your gift basket may include: stationery, a book of stamps, pens, pencils, herbal potpourris for the drawer and closet (see instructions on page 70), soap case, a small sewing kit in a decorative tin, and a laundry bag. (Make the laundry bag from a purchased pillow case and 1-1/2 yards of cording. Simply make a casing at the top of the pillow case and run the cording through it. Remember to knot the ends of the cord so they don't slip into the casing.)

For that special guy:

Include the recipe for hot toddy (see page 7 for recipe) accompanied with bagged spices and cinnamon sticks, mug, jar of pepper jelly (see page 63 for recipe), crackers, monogrammed hankies, a deck of cards, a pocket calendar, and men's sachets for drawers and closets (see page 70 for instructions).

For the romantic:

Your gift basket may include potpourri and herbal bath sachets (instructions for heart sachets on page 70), embroidered heart ornament (see instructions on page 67), a tussie-mussie or nosegay (see instructions on page 66), a romantic novel specially gift-wrapped (see instructions for gift wrap on page 73), a small wooden hand mirror decorated with buttons, ribbons, and decorative trims, a loaf of beribboned lemon-nut bread (recipe on page 28), and herbal tea bags and the accompanying list of their "remedies".

Men's Sachets

Tuck a few of these sachets in his drawers or suitcase. They really refresh the closet too!

Fabric and supply requirements:
—2 - 3-1/2" x 3-1/2" squares of plaid or pin-striped fabric
—4 teaspoons of herbal spice potpourri
—Pinking shears

Instructions:
1. Cut 2 squares, 3-1/2" x 3-1/2" from plaid or pin-striped fabric.
2. Lay the squares *wrong* sides together. Stitch a 1/2" seam through both thicknesses, around the square, leaving a 2" opening on one side.
3. Fill the square with potpourri.
4. Top-stitch the opening closed.
5. Bundle 3 or 4 sachets together with a ribbon—ready for gift giving.

Herbal Teas and Bath Sachets

The following herbal tea "remedies" are old remedies for minor aches and pains. For more reading on herbs consult the ***Illustrated Encyclopedia of Herbs***, Rodale Press, Emmaus, Pennsylvania.

Herbal teas:
—Chamomile tea - good aid for digestion, upset stomach, and headache.
—Peppermint tea - good for the flue or cold, and helps insomnia.
—Lemon verbena tea - aids digestion and helps reduce a fever.
—Rosehip tea - is a great source of vitamin C (ounce for ounce, more vitamin C than orange juice.)

Herbal bath sachets:

Include an herbal bath sachet in your gift basket. A refreshing herbal bath is said to relieve stress and tension. Try one for yourself:

Supplies:
—Scraps of unbleached muslin
—Scraps of ribbon, twine, or string
—An herbal mixture of any of the following:
Chamomile flowers
Hyssop
Jasmine flowers
Lemon peel
Lavender flowers
Rose petals
—An ounce, or so, of rolled oats for bulk and to soften the water and skin.

Directions:
1. Cut 2 rectangles 3" x 5" from muslin. Stitch 1/2" seam around three sides, leaving a "short" side open. Do not turn right sides out. Simply pink the edges on all 4 sides with pinking shears.
2. Place herbal mixture (about 1/2 cup) into bag.
3. Tie securely with twine, ribbon, or string.
4. Attach an instructions tag:
"Steep bath sachet in hot tub water several minutes before bathing. Squeeze out excess water from sachet and save for one more bath."

Decorative Gift Wrap

Decorative gift wrap with a feminine touch:

Make your gift giving even more special by adding a few decorative touches to your packages. Collect ribbons, artificial berries, gilded nuts and pods, ribbon rosettes, and dried herbs and flowers throughout the year.

Save decorative trims from old corsages and centerpieces. Store these "treasures" in a clear plastic box so you have easy access to them.

Remember, it doesn't necessarily have to be Christmas for you to wrap your gifts in a special way!

Supplies:

—Hot glue gun ("cool" glue gun works best)
—Sprigs of artificial garland
—Dried herbs and flowers
—Ribbons and ribbon rosettes
—Gilded artificial berries
—Gilded nuts and pods
—Roll of white wrapping paper

Instructions:

1. Wrap present in white paper.
2. Tie ribbon around package. Tie plain bow on package.
3. Make a "base" for your arrangement by hot glueing sprigs of garland around the base of the bow.
4. Next, glue dried flowers and herbs to the base.
5. Now, glue the pods, nuts, berries, and/or ribbon rosettes to the arrangement.

Decorative gift wrap with a masculine touch:

Supplies:

—Lightweight brown postal wrap
—Hot glue gun ("cool" glue gun works best)
—Sprigs of artificial garland
—Dried herbs and flowers
—Acorns, nuts, and pods
—Artificial red berries
—Ribbon

Instructions:

Follow the instructions for "gift wrap with a feminine touch", except, use, natural colored nuts, acorns, pods, herbs, and flowers.

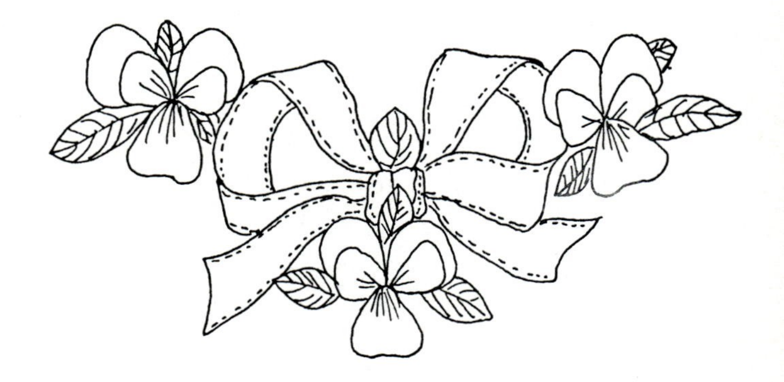

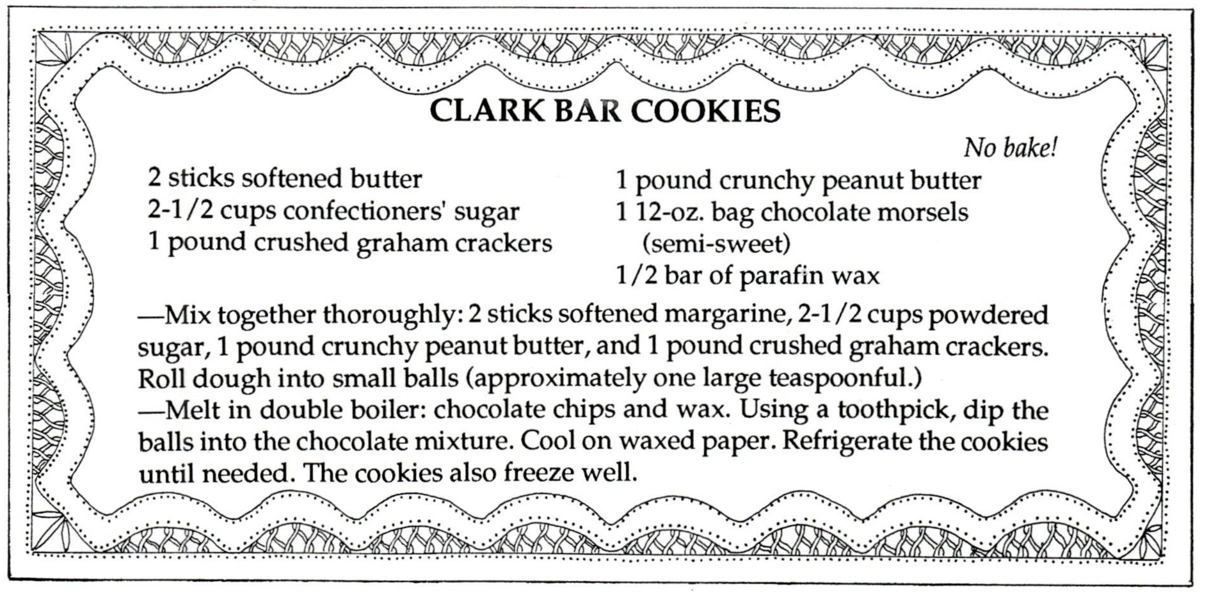

CLARK BAR COOKIES

No bake!

2 sticks softened butter
2-1/2 cups confectioners' sugar
1 pound crushed graham crackers
1 pound crunchy peanut butter
1 12-oz. bag chocolate morsels (semi-sweet)
1/2 bar of parafin wax

—Mix together thoroughly: 2 sticks softened margarine, 2-1/2 cups powdered sugar, 1 pound crunchy peanut butter, and 1 pound crushed graham crackers. Roll dough into small balls (approximately one large teaspoonful.)
—Melt in double boiler: chocolate chips and wax. Using a toothpick, dip the balls into the chocolate mixture. Cool on waxed paper. Refrigerate the cookies until needed. The cookies also freeze well.

Diagonal Scrap Nine-Patch Quilt

finished size: 68" x 96"

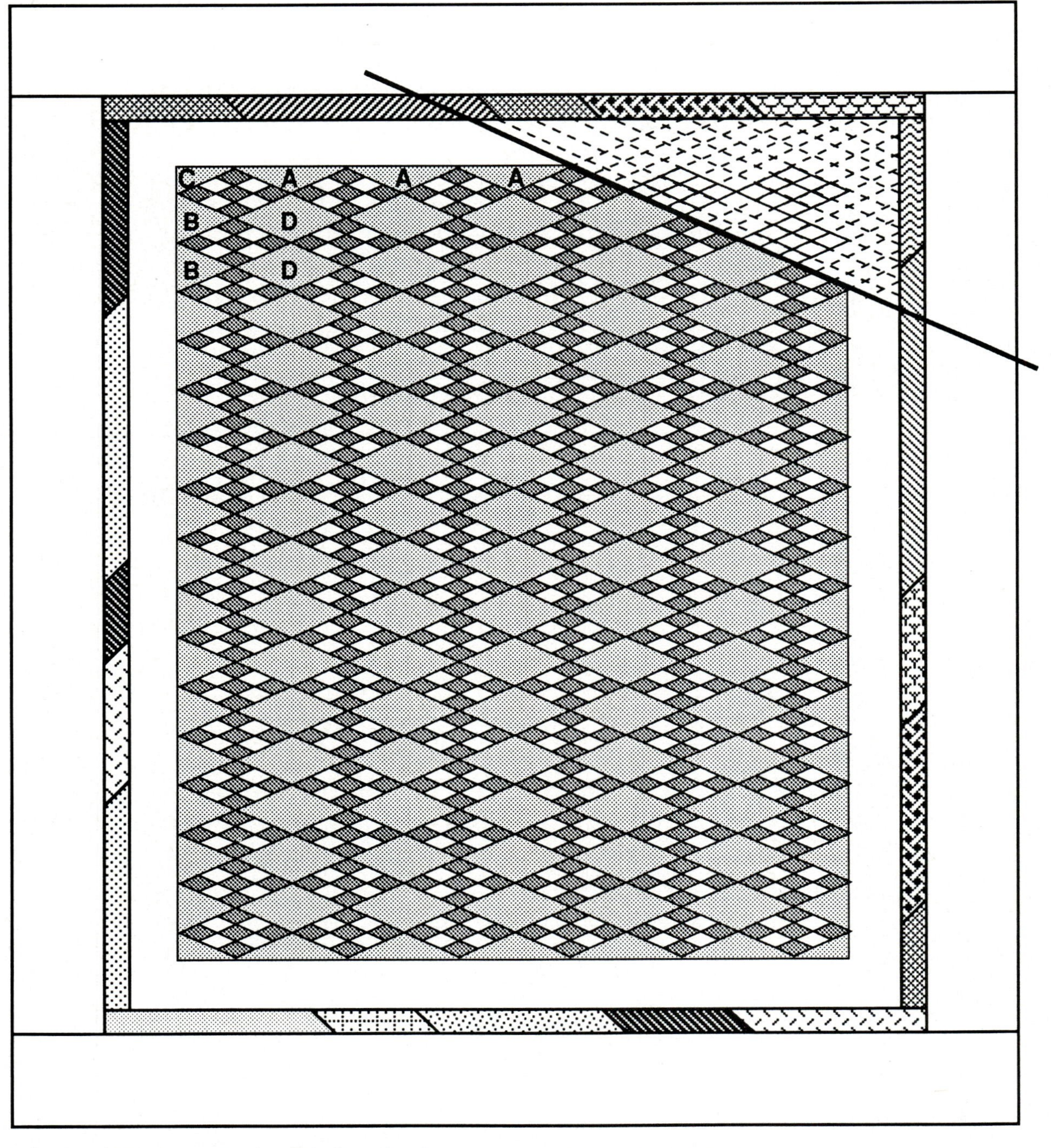

Block size: 4-1/2" wide diamond, finished
Number of blocks: 96 pieced, 75 spacer
Setting: diagonal

Fabric requirements:
— 38 - 2" wide strips of various medium/dark to dark fabrics (includes pieced border)
— 24 - 2" wide strips of various light to medium/light fabrics
— 5-1/4 yards setting, first and third borders, and binding fabric
— 5-3/4 yards backing fabric
— 72" x 100" batting

Pre-wash all fabrics. Quick-cutting and piecing techniques are used whenever possible. Use a rotary cutter and plastic template ruler with a 60° angle marked on it. Trace, cut, and transfer all markings for Templates A, B, and C.

Cutting instructions for the diagonal nine-patches:
1. Cut 38 - 2" wide strips of medium/dark to dark
2. Cut 24 - 2" wide strips of light to medium/light
3. Sub-cut *all* of the strips from #1 and #2 in half diagonally using a 60° angle. See Diagram 1.

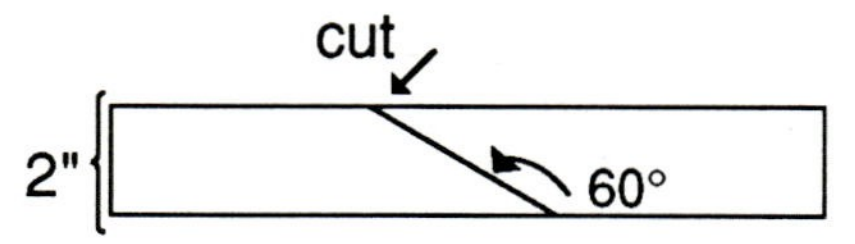

Diagram 1.

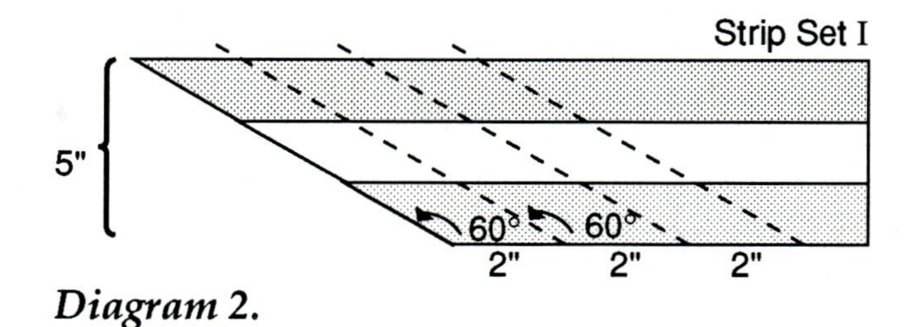

Diagram 2.

Sewing strip sets I and II:
1. For strip sets I: Select two "dark" strips and one "light" strip. Stagger them as in Diagram 2. Seam accurate 1/4" wide seams. Press light to dark on the wrong side. Flip strip set over and press again on top to remove any "tucks". Make sure the strip set is 5" wide. Make 24 strip sets in this fashion.
2. For strip sets II: Select two "light" strips and one "dark" strip. Stagger them as previously done for strip sets. Stitch an accurate 1/4" seam. Press. The strip set must measure 5" wide. See Diagram 3. Make 12 of these strip sets. Set the leftover medium/dark to dark strips aside for use in piecing the pieced border.

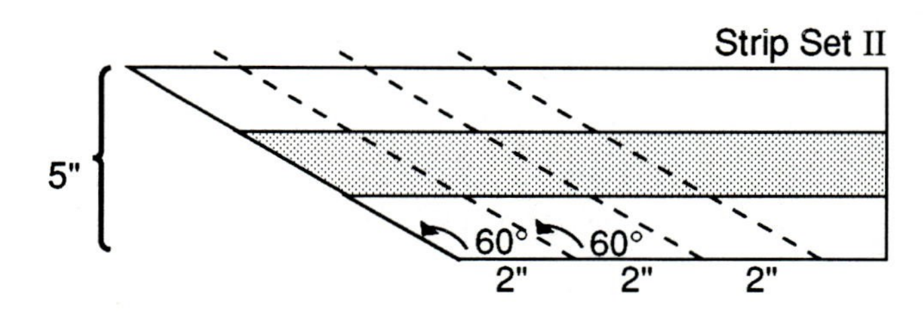

Diagram 3.

Sub-cutting strip sets I and II:
1. Sub-cut strip sets I and II at 2" intervals. Use the 60° angle on the template ruler as a guide. Make sure the 60° angle runs along the bottom edge while cutting. After cutting a couple of pieces, make sure you still have an accurate 60° angle. See Diagrams #2 and #3. Cut up all the strip sections in this manner.

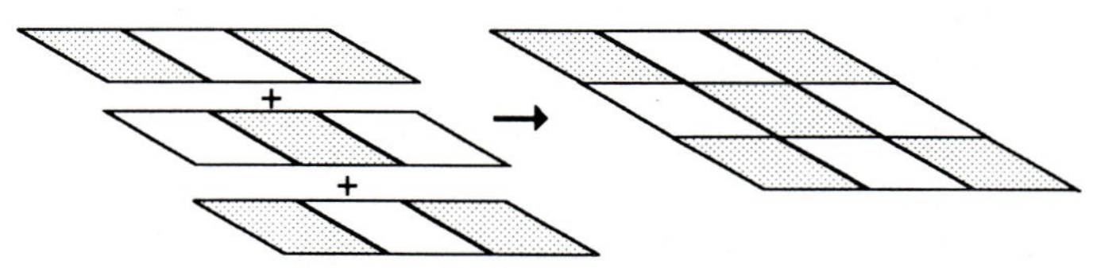

*Diagram 4. *Pin the strip sections before stitching, matching up the seamlines.*

Piecing diagonal nine-patches:
1. To piece the nine-patch diamonds, follow Diagram 4. Piece 96 nine-patches.
2. "Proof" the diamonds by laying the template ruler over the pieced diamonds. The side angles should be 60° and the diamonds should be 5" wide. See Diagram 5.

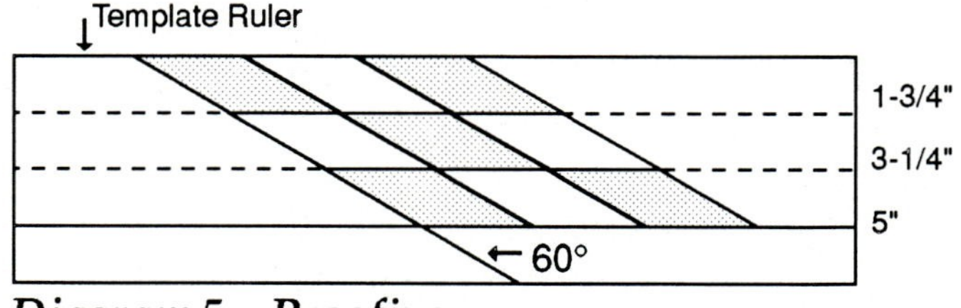

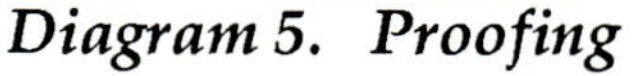
Diagram 5. Proofing

Cutting setting fabric:
1. Cut 13 strips 5" wide. Sub-cut (see Diagram 6) 75 pieces D (spacers), **NOTE:* Check to make sure the 60° angle is accurate after cutting a couple of pieces.
2. Cut 2 strips 3-1/8" wide. Using template A, cut a total of 10 pieces A from the strip. From the

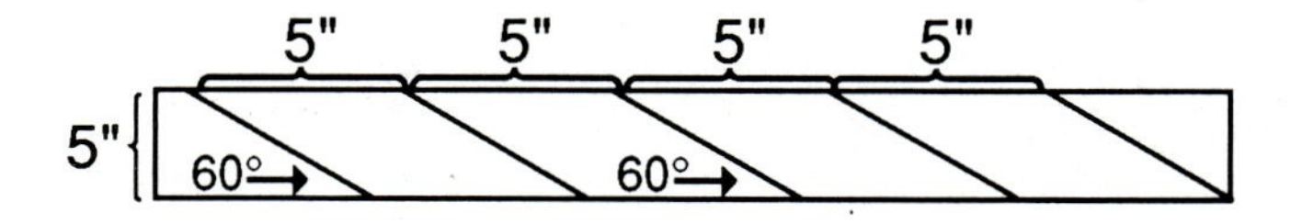

Diagram 6.

remainder of the strip cut, using template C, 2 pieces regular and 2 pieces mirror image for a total of 4 pieces C.
3. Cut 3 strips 5-1/4" wide. Either use template B or use method illustrated in Diagram 7. Cut a total of 30 pieces B from these strips.

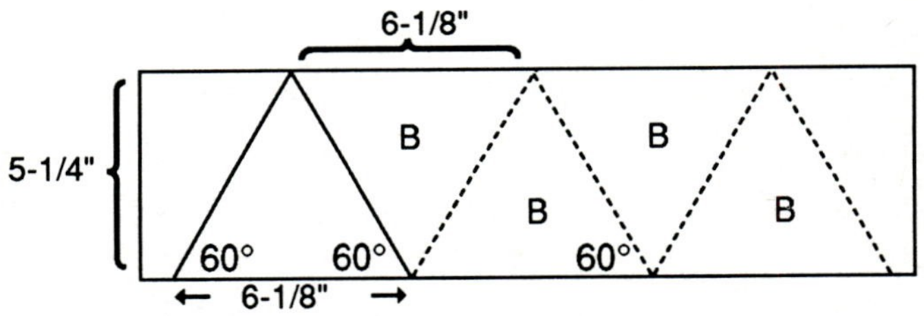

Diagram 7.

Cutting borders and binding:
1. Follow Diagram 8 for cutting first border, third border, and binding along the straight of the remaining setting fabric. At least 88" in length are required. First border: 4 strips 2-1/2" by length of fabric. Third border: 4 strips 5-1/2" by the length of fabric. Binding: 4 strips 2-1/4" by the length of the fabric.

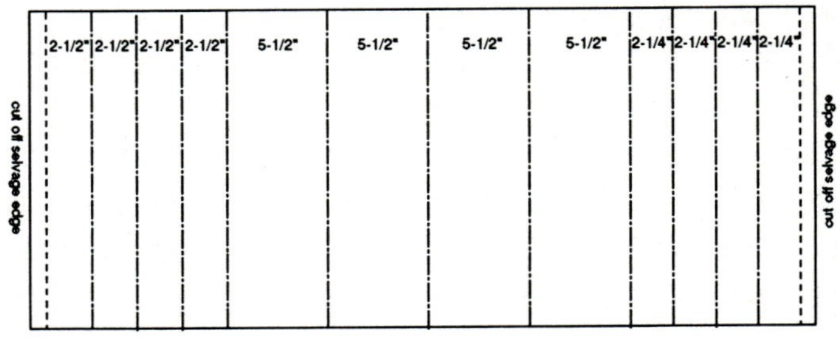

Diagram 8

Quilt layout:
1. Layout the nine-patches and setting blocks according to the "whole quilt diagram". Pin and stitch together the diagonal rows. Press towards setting blocks.
2. After all diagonal rows are stitched, pin and stitch the rows together, butting seams. Add corner pieces C last.
3. Retrieve pre-cut 2-1/2" wide border strips. Refer to General Instructions under "Bordering a quilt". Pin and stitch these borders accordingly. Press.
4. Pieced border. Retrieve the left over medium/dark to dark strips. Cut and piece this border randomly. Vary in length of the cut strips. Make border strips long enough for the side borders, and the top and bottom borders respectively. Pin and stitch borders as previously done in #3.
5. Retrieve the pre-cut 5-1/2" wide border strips. Pin and stitch borders in the same manner as in #3.

Finishing:
Refer to Whole quilt diagram for quilting suggestions.

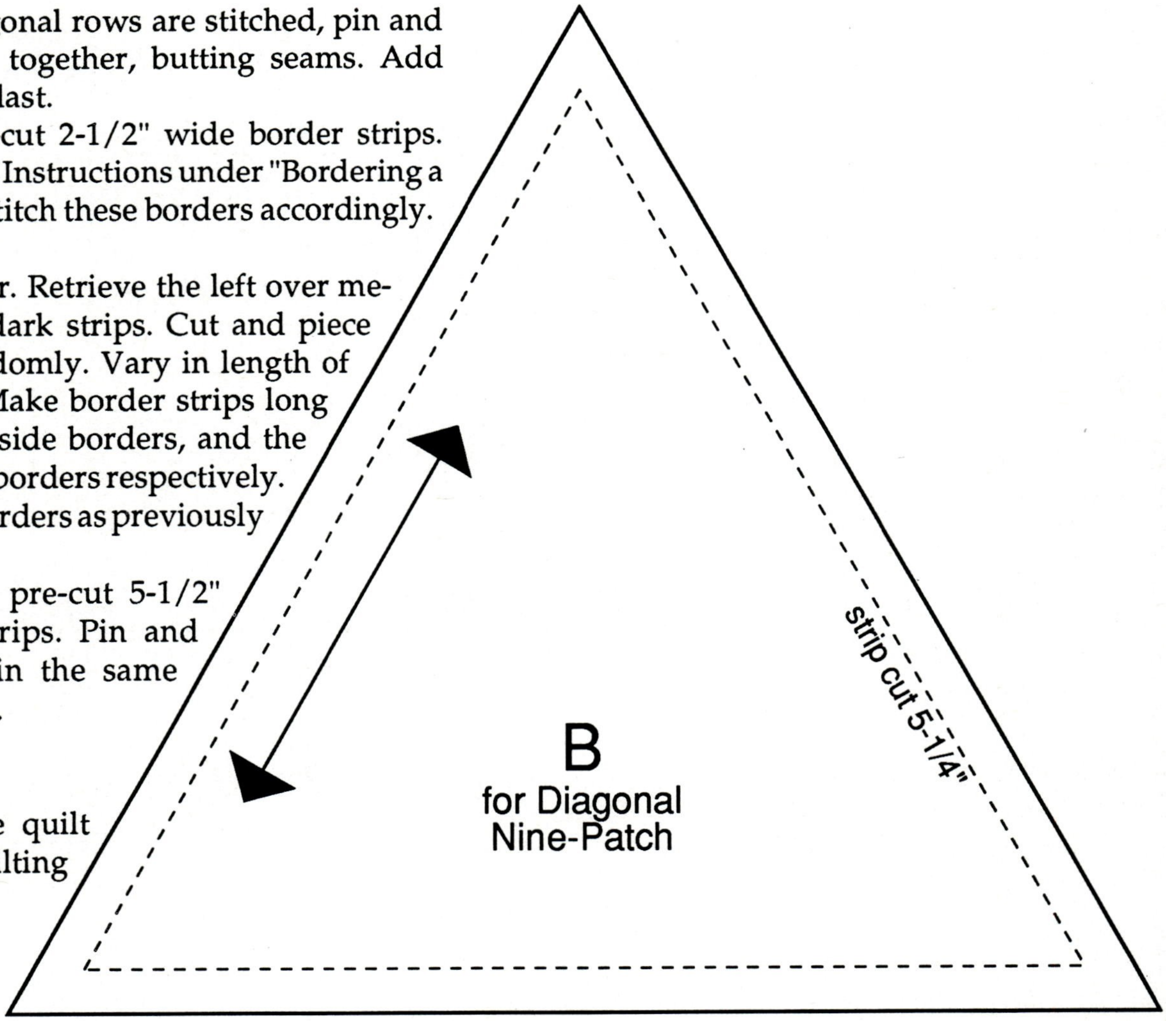

KELLI'S PEANUT BRITTLE

Fast: 8-10 minutes total
Microwave Recipe

1 cup sugar
1/2 cup white corn syrup
1 cup peanuts (roasted, salted)
1 teaspoon butter
1 teaspoon vanilla flavoring
1 teaspoon baking soda

—In 1-1/2 quart casserole stir together sugar and syrup. Microwave on high for 4 minutes. Stir in peanuts. Microwave on high for 3 minutes, until the mixture is light brown. Add butter and vanilla to mixture, blending well. Microwave on high for 1 minute. Add baking soda and gently stir until light and foamy. Pour mixture onto lightly greased cookie sheet. Cool 1/2 - 1 hour. When cool, break up and put into airtight container.

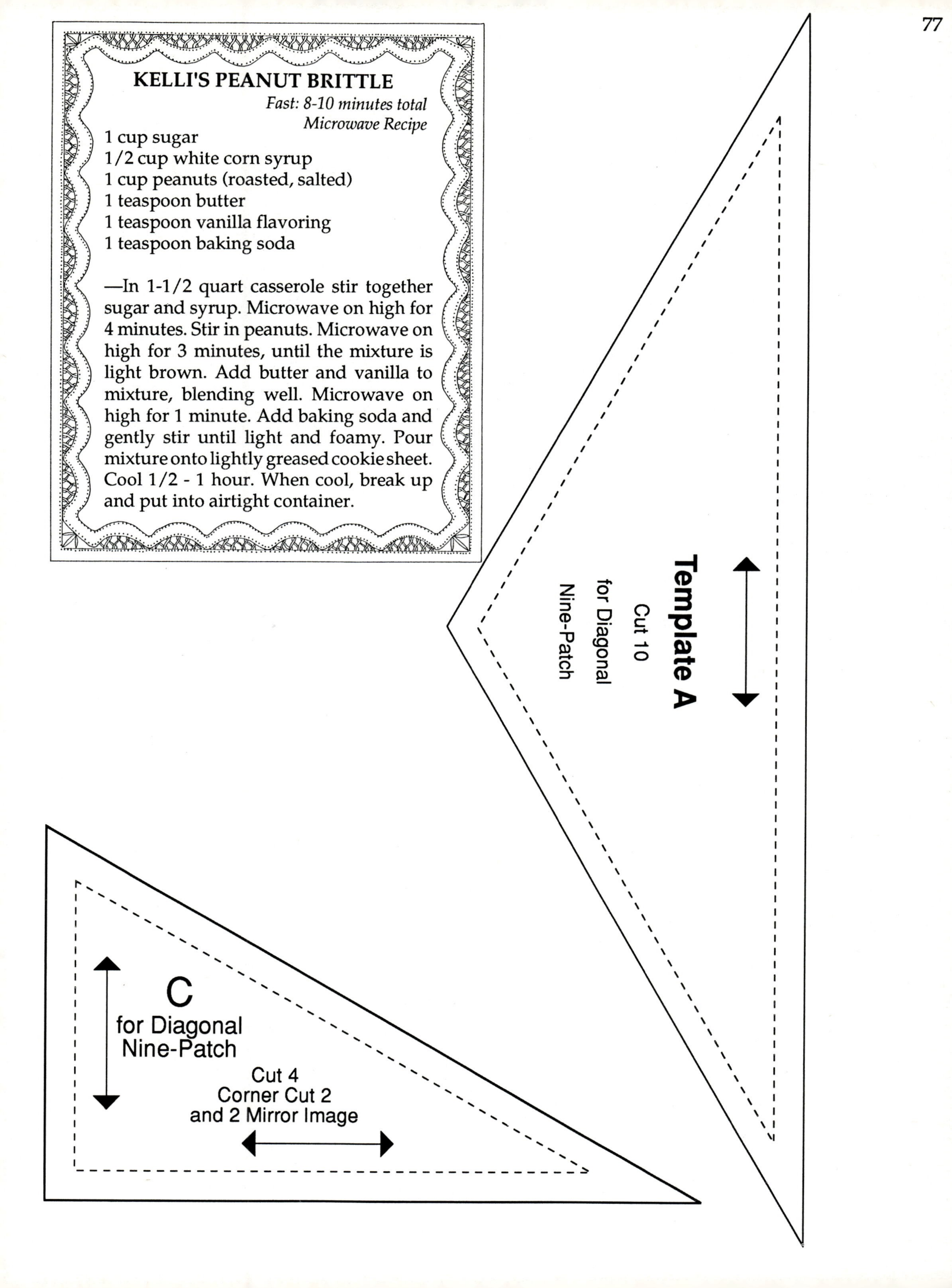

Country Crossroads

87-1/2" x 105"

color photo on page 56

Block size: Main block finished size: 10-1/2" x 10-1/2"
Spacer star block finished size: 7" x 10-1/2"
Spacer block finished size: 7" x 7"
Number of blocks: Main 30, Spacer star - 20, and spacer - 49
Setting: Straight

Pre-wash all fabrics. Cut Template 1 from template plastic.
For the purpose of conserving fabric, it is best to cut the entire quilt out all at once. Please label each pile as you cut. Keep the main block, star spacer, and spacer pieces separated from each other.

Fabric requirements:
— 7-1/2 yards background
— 5/8 yard of 10 different red fabrics
—3/8 yard of 10 different green fabrics
— 1/4 yard of 8 different tan fabrics
— 3/4 yard binding fabric
— 6-1/2 yards backing fabric
— 90" x 108" batting

Cutting instructions:
From background fabric cut:
—10 strips 1-1/2" wide (for nine-patch in center of main block)
— 8 strips 2-5/8" wide (for half-square triangles E1E2 in main block)
— 7 strips 4" wide (for double half-square triangles F2DF2 in main block)
— 12 strips 2-1/4" wide (for star spacers and main block)
— 11 strips 2-1/4" wide (for spacer blocks)
— 10 strips 11" wide (for spacer block)
— 6 strips 4-3/4" wide (for border triangles)
From each of the ten red fabrics cut:
— 3 strips 2-1/4" wide (for star spacer and main blocks)
— 1 strip 1-1/2" wide (for nine-patch in main block)
— 1 strip 4" wide. Sub-cut 2-4" squares from each

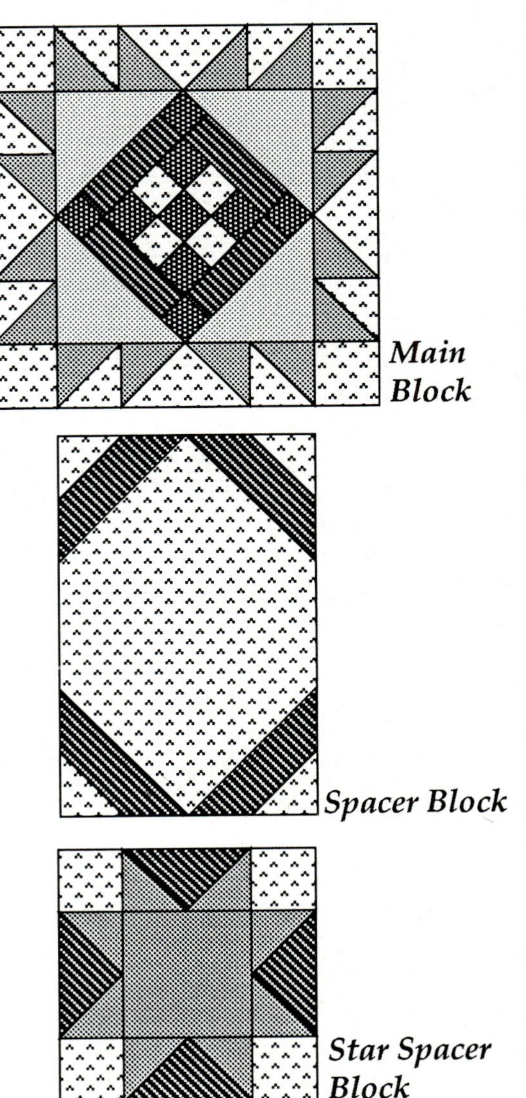

Diagram 1.

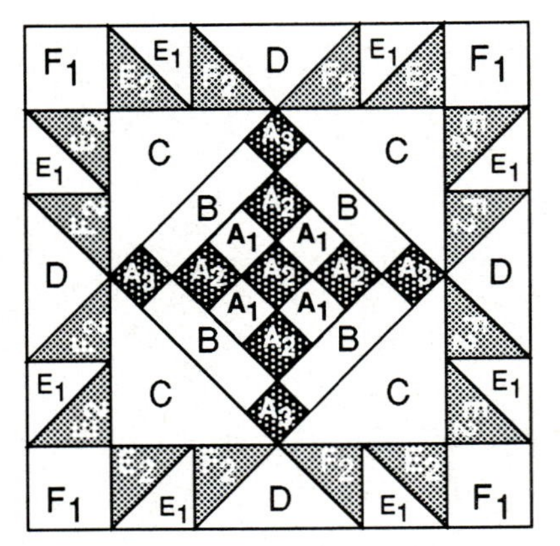

Diagram 2.

strip to yield a total of 20 - 4" squares. Set these aside for star spacer pieces I. Trim the remainder of each 4" strip down to a 2-1/4" wide strip and a 1-1/2" wide strip. Place these strips according to their width, with the other strips previously cut directly above.

— 1 strip 2-5/8" wide (for main block)

From each of 7 different red fabrics cut:

— 1 strip 4-3/4" wide (for borders)

From each of the 8 different tan fabrics cut:

— 1 strip 4-3/8" wide

From each of 5 different green fabrics cut:

— 1 square 4-3/4" x 4-3/4" (set aside for border)

From each of the 10 different green fabrics cut:

— 2 strips 4-3/8" wide (used in all blocks)

Construction of main blocks:

Nine-patch construction

1. Retrieve the 20 - 1-1/2" wide strips (including the strips cut down from the 4" strip) of red.
2. Sub-cut 12 squares, 1-1/2" x 1-1/2" (pieces A3) from each of the full strips of the 10 different fabrics. Set aside. Yield: 120 pieces A3.
3. Cut the remainder of each strip in half, along the short side, to yield 20 strips approximately 12" long.
4. Cut a 6" long piece from each of the remaining 1-1/2" strips. Yield: 10 strips 6" long.
5. Retrieve the 10 - 1-1/2" wide strips of background. Sub-cut these strips: 10 strips 12" long and 20 strips 6" long.
6. Pair the strips up in *like* fabric "sets". See Diagram 3. You will have 10 sets of each. The strip sets are 3-1/2" wide. Press the light towards dark. Sub-cut the 12" long strip sets into six 1-1/2" sections. See Diagram 4. Cut the short strip set into three 1-1/2" sections. See Diagram 4.
7. Proceed to make three nine-patch blocks from each of the matching strip sections. Yield: 3 nine-patch from each color, for a total of 30 in all. Blocks should measure 3-1/2" x 3-1/2". See Diagram 5.

Adding pieces B to nine-patch:

1. Retrieve the pre-cut strips of green.
2. Sub-cut 98 squares 4-3/8" x 4-3/8" from the strips. You will cut up one strip from each color. (It depends on the width of your fabric whether

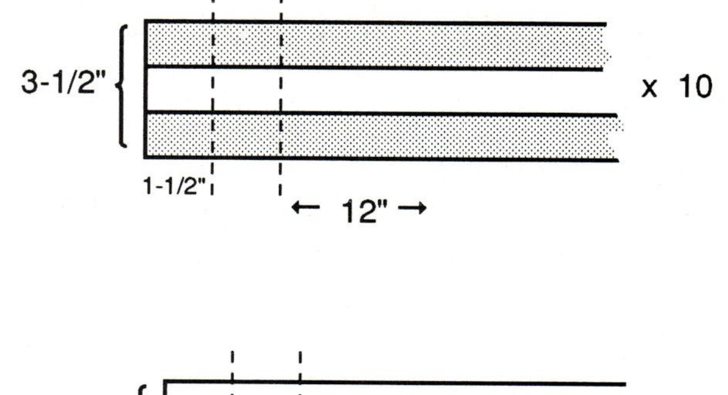

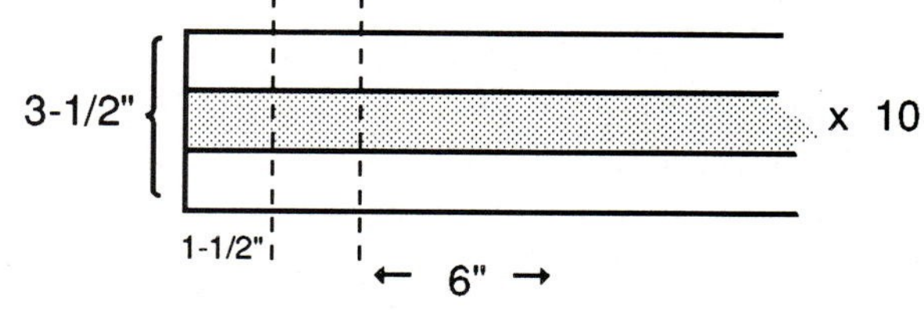

Diagram 3 and 4.

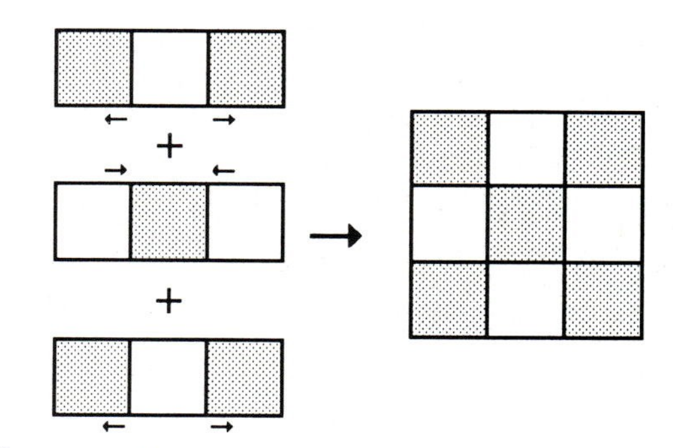

Diagram 5.

you will need the next strip at this time.) Make sure you have all 98 squares pre-cut before proceeding. Set these aside for use in the spacer blocks.

3. Trim the remaining strips down to 4" wide. Sub-cut 8 pieces 2-1/4" x 4" (pieces D) from each fabric. Yield: 80 pieces D. Set these aside for the star spacer block.

4. Cut the leftover strips down to 3-1/2" wide. Sub-cut 12 pieces 1-1/2" x 3-1/2" (pieces B) from each fabric. Yield: 120 pieces B.

5. Retrieve the 120 pre-cut 1-1/2" square pieces A3 of red fabric. With one of your nine-patches in front of you, pick 4 squares A3 of the same fabric as in the nine-patch. Pick 4 pieces of green (1-1/2" x 3-1/2"). Follow Diagram 6. Sew a piece B to either side of nine-patch. Press seam away from center. Sew a square A3 to either side of the 2 remaining B's. Press toward center. Seam these sections to nine-patch. Press.

6. Repeat for all 30 blocks. Blocks should measure 5-1/2" x 5-1/2".

Adding triangles C:

1. Retrieve the 8 pre-cut tan strips. Sub-cut these strips into 8 - 4-3/8" x 4-3/8" squares per strip. Sub-cut these squares in half diagonally once to yield: 16 triangles C per strip. Total yield: 128 triangles. (Important note * see General Instructions for diagonal sub-cutting.)

2. Seam a triangle C to either side of the nine-patch. *Note: You may want to finger press the triangle in half and the block in half to find center points for lining up the triangle on the block. Press without stretching. Seam a triangle C to remaining sides. Press. The block should now measure 7-1/2" x 7-1/2". Repeat for all 30 blocks. Refer to Diagram 7 for illustration of triangles C.

Making main block points:

1. Retrieve the 8 pre-cut 2-5/8" wide strips of background. Sub-cut these strips into 120 2-5/8" squares.

2. Retrieve the 10 pre-cut 2-5/8" wide strips of red fabric. Sub-cut these strips to yield 12 - 2-5/8" squares per fabric selection or a total of 120 - 2-5/8" squares.

3. Refer back to the General Instructions for "Making half-square triangles". Follow exactly.

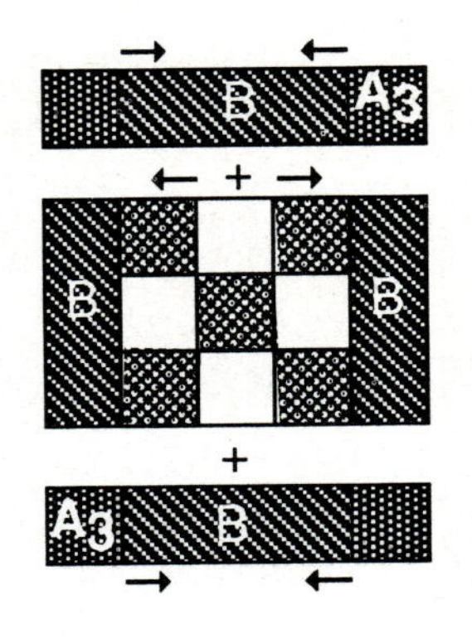

Diagram 6.

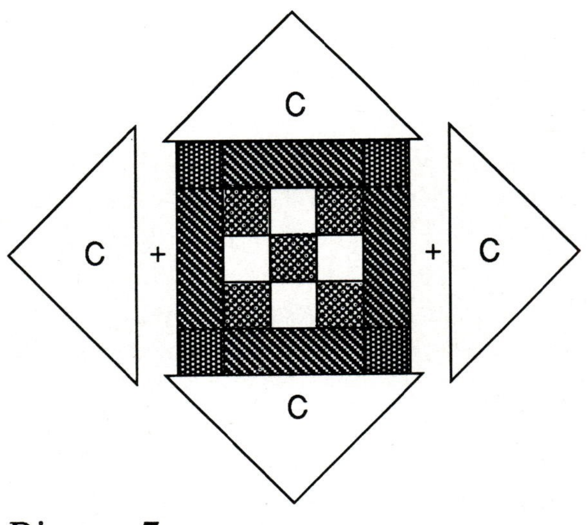

Diagram 7.

"Proof" the half-square triangles to be 2-1/4" x 2-1/4". Yield: 240 . Set aside.

4. Retrieve the 7 pre-cut 4" wide strips of background fabric. Sub-cut these strips to total 120 - 2-1/4" x 4" (pieces D). Set aside.

5. Retrieve the 3 pre-cut 2-1/4" wide strips of each of the red fabrics. Total 30.

6. Cut a total of 40 - 2-1/4" x 2-1/4" squares from each fabric selection. **Important: Set 16 squares from *each* fabric aside for later use in star spacer block.

7. Draw a diagonal line on the wrong side of all the 2-1/4" squares from step #6 above. (Except for the ones put aside.)

8. Using the 120 pre-cut background 2-1/4" x 4" pieces and the squares from step #7, follow "Making double half-square triangles" in the General Instructions Finished pieces should measure 2-1/4" x 4". Set aside. x 120.

9. Retrieve the 7 pre-cut 2-1/4" wide strips of background. Sub-cut these strips to yield: 120 - 2-1/4" x 2-1/4" squares (F1).

10. Assemble the blocks following Diagram 8. Assemble all 30 blocks. The arrows show pressing direction.

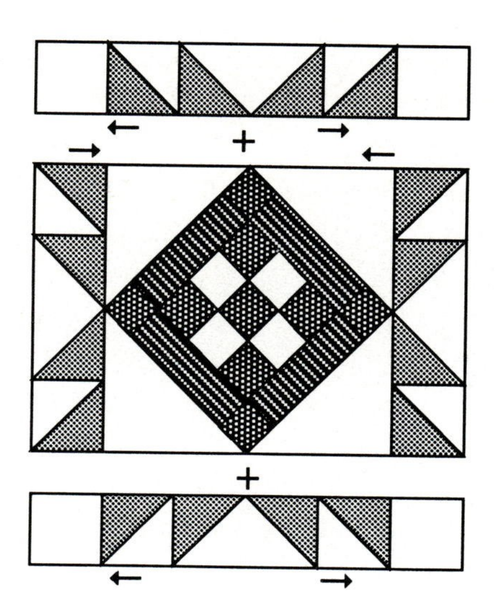

Diagram 8.

Spacer star blocks: 20 blocks (See Diagram 1)

1. Retrieve the following pre-cut pieces:
— 20 squares of red 4" x 4" (I)
— 160 squares of red 2-1/4" x 2-1/4"
— 5 strips of background 2-1/4" wide
— 80 rectangles of green 2-1/4" x 4" (D)

2. Sub-cut 80 - 2-1/4" x 2-1/4" squares from the 5 strips of background.

3. Draw a diagonal line on the wrong side of the 160 squares of red (2-1/4" x 2-1/4"). With these squares and the 80 green rectangles, proceed to "Making double half-square triangles" in the General Instructions. Make 80 (Use the same red fabric on either side of the piece. However, vary the green fabric selection.)

4. Assemble the 20 star spacer blocks according to Diagram 9. Press seams in the arrow direction. Set aside.

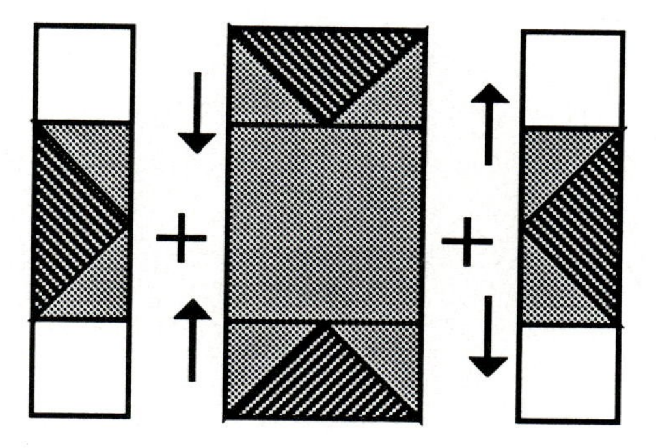

Diagram 9.

Spacer blocks: 49 blocks (See Diagram 1)
1. Retrieve the following pre-cut pieces:
— 98 squares of green 4-3/8" x 4-3/8" (H)
— 10 strips of background fabric 11" wide
— 11 strips of background fabric 2-1/4" wide.
2. Sub-cut 49 pieces - 7-1/2" x 11" from the 11" strips for pieces G. Place Template 1 on the rectangles (only layer 2 at a time) and trim corners off. Repeat for all 49.
3. Sub-cut 196 - 2-1/4" x 2-1/4" squares from the 11 strips of background. Draw a diagonal line on the wrong side of all squares. Place a square, right sides together, on the opposite corners of each green 4-3/8" x 4-3/8" square. See Diagram 10.
4. Stitch *on* the drawn diagonal line. Trim excess fabric, leaving a 1/4" seam allowance. See Diagram 11. Press the background piece out. Now carefully cut the squares in half diagonally once as in Diagram 12. Repeat for all 98 squares. Yield: 196 triangle corners.
5. Pin and seam a triangle corner to opposite sides of background pieces G. Press out. Add the other corners. Press. The block should measure 7-1/2" x 11".

Quilt assembly:
1. Lay out the quilt according to lay out Diagram 16. Pin and sew block/spacer rows according to Diagram 13 and spacer/star spacer rows according to Diagram 14.
2. Pin and seam rows together, pressing as you go.

Pieced border:
1. Retrieve the following pre-cut pieces:
— 7 strips of various reds 4-3/4" wide
— 5 squares of various greens 4-3/4" x 4-3/4"
— 6 strips of background fabric 4-3/4" wide
2. Sub-cut 51 - 4-3/4" x 4-3/4" squares from the red strips. Sub-cut diagonally twice, all 51 squares to yield: 204 border triangles.
3. Sub-cut 46 - 4-3/4" x 4-3/4" squares from the background strips. Sub-cut diagonally twice , all 46 squares to yield: 184 border triangles.

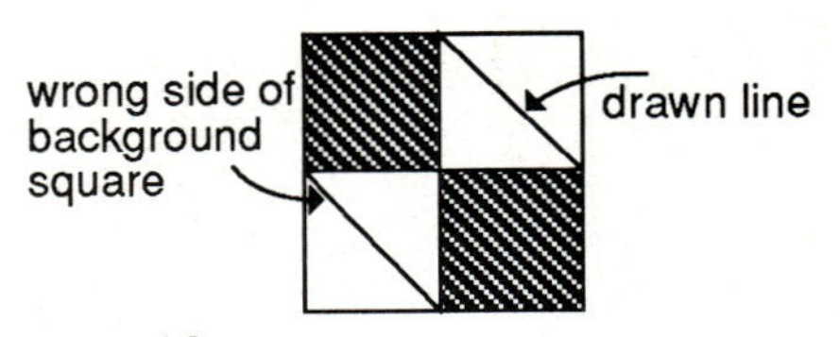

Diagram 10.

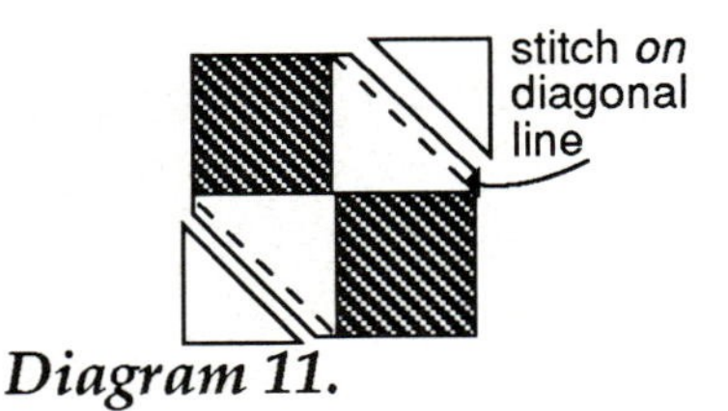

Diagram 11.

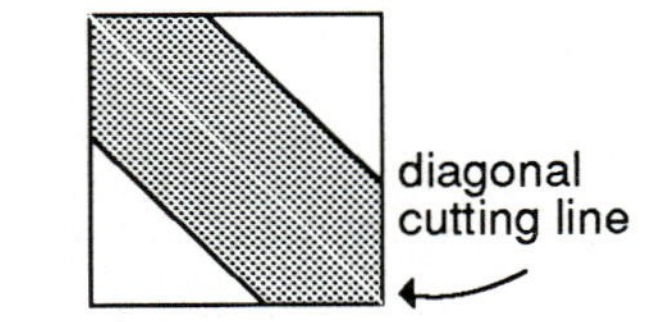

Diagram 12.

Main Block	Spacer	Main Block	Spacer	Main Block	Spacer	Main Block	Spacer	Main Block

Diagram 13.

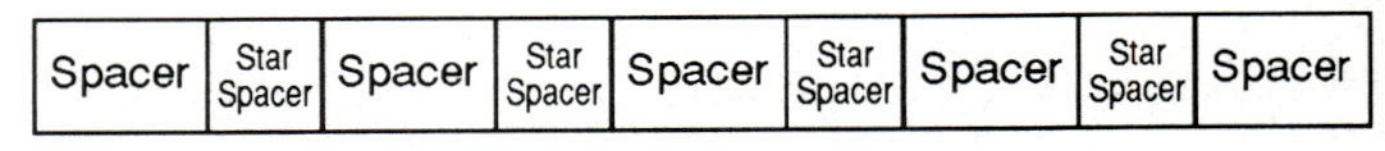

Diagram 14.

4. Other pieces needed for border (cut from scraps):
— 4 - 2-5/8 x 2-5/8" squares of *background*. Sub-cut in half diagonally once for 8 pieces J.
— 2 - 4-3/8" x 4-3/8" squares of *background*. Sub-cut in half diagonally once for 4 pieces L.
— 6 - 2-5/8" x 2-5/8" squares of various *reds*. Sub-cut in half diagonally once to yield: 12 pieces K.
5. Refer to layout diagram 16. Piece side borders first. Check the stitching against the sewn quilt top to make sure the border strips are going to match up. You must press after each triangle is added in order for the border to lay flat. Pin and sew border to quilt. Press.

6. Refer to Diagram 15 for piecing corner blocks which are attached to right and left sides of the top and bottom borders. These blocks should be 4" x 4".
7. Piece top and bottom borders, adding the corner blocks (see Diagram 16). Pin and sew top and bottom border to quilt.

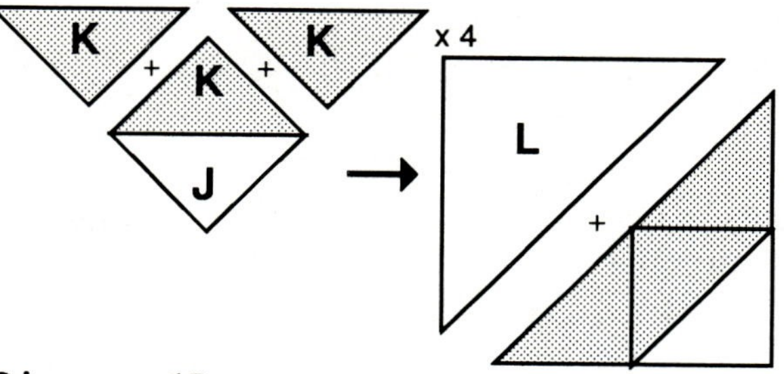

Diagram 15.

Finishing the quilt:
1. Quilting suggestions: The main blocks were quilted close to the seamlines and an X was quilted diagonally through the checkerboard center. The spacer stars were quilted close to the seamlines and a square was tipped diagonally in the center square.
2. Prepare the quilt backing: Remove selvage edges from fabric. Cut 2 pieces 3 yards long (check with your quilt size before cutting). Seam pieces together along the long side. It is necessary to add another side strip to make the backing wide enough. Use the remaining fabric to cut and piece strips for side.
3. Mark quilting lines. Refer to General Instructions for layering up the quilt, hand or machine quilting, and binding. (Cut 10 strips 2-1/4" wide for binding.)

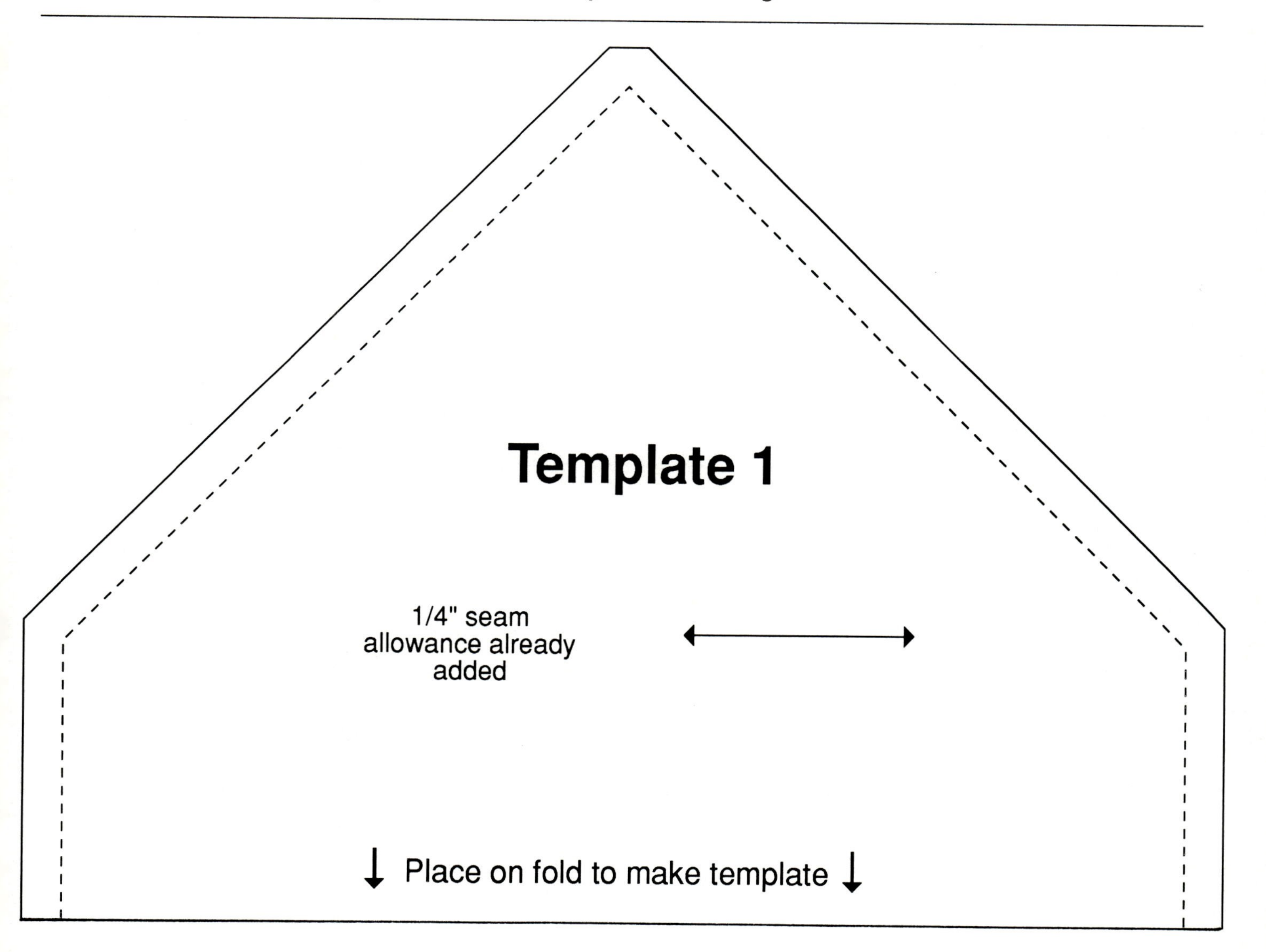

Main Block	Spacer	Main Block	Spacer	Main Block	Spacer	Main Block	Spacer	Main Block
Spacer	Spacer Star	Spacer	Spacer Star	Spacer	Spacer Star	Spacer	Spacer Star	Spacer
Main Block	Spacer	Main Block	Spacer	Main Block	Spacer	Main Block	Spacer	Main Block
Spacer	Spacer Star	Spacer	Spacer Star	Spacer	Spacer Star	Spacer	Spacer Star	Spacer
Main Block	Spacer	Main Block	Spacer	Main Block	Spacer	Main Block	Spacer	Main Block
Spacer	Spacer Star	Spacer	Spacer Star	Spacer	Spacer Star	Spacer	Spacer Star	Spacer
Main Block	Spacer	Main Block	Spacer	Main Block	Spacer	Main Block	Spacer	Main Block
Spacer	Spacer Star	Spacer	Spacer Star	Spacer	Spacer Star	Spacer	Spacer Star	Spacer
Main Block	Spacer	Main Block	Spacer	Main Block	Spacer	Main Block	Spacer	Main Block
Spacer	Spacer Star	Spacer	Spacer Star	Spacer	Spacer Star	Spacer	Spacer Star	Spacer
Main Block	Spacer	Main Block	Spacer	Main Block	Spacer	Main Block	Spacer	Main Block

Diagram 16.

Scrappy Stars Quilt

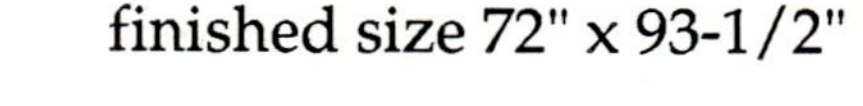
finished size 72" x 93-1/2"

Block size: finished 21-1/2" x 21-1/2"
Number of blocks: 6
Setting: straight

Pre-wash all fabrics. The Scrappy Stars was pieced to have a scrappy, non-planned look. Don't be afraid to use plaids, stripds, small, and large scale prints in this quilt. This pattern has been written for the quick-cutting and piecing techniques. Please use a rotary cutter and plastic template ruler.

Fabric requirements:
—30 medium/dark to dark scrap strips - 2" x width of fabric
— 20 medium/'light to light scrap strips - 2" x width of fabric
— 4-1/2 yards setting fabric (includes last border and binding)
— 1/3 yard first border fabric
— 1/2 yard second border fabric
— 5-1/2 yards backing fabric
— 75" x 96" batting

Cutting instructions for the stars
(left overs will be used for the pieced border):
1. Cut 30 strips of dark, medium/dark fabric 2" wide.
2. Cut 20 strips of light, medium/light fabric 2" wide.
3. Sub-cut all the strips in half diagonally at a 45° angle. See Diagram 1. *While cutting these strips in half, also cut one or two single diamonds from the strip. Lay your template ruler so the 45° angle is along the bottom edge of the strip and the 2" line is on the cut angled edge. Cut the diamonds at 2" intervals. You need about 60 single diamonds altogether from all your different fabrics. (Put these aside for later use in the pieced border.)

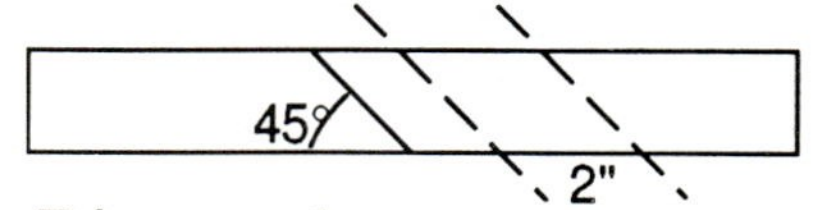

Diagram 1.

Stitching strip sets:
1. Randomly pair up the cut strips into strip sets 1 and 2 as shown in Diagram 2. Stitch 1/4" seams. Carefully press all seams in one direction. The strip sets must be 5" wide.

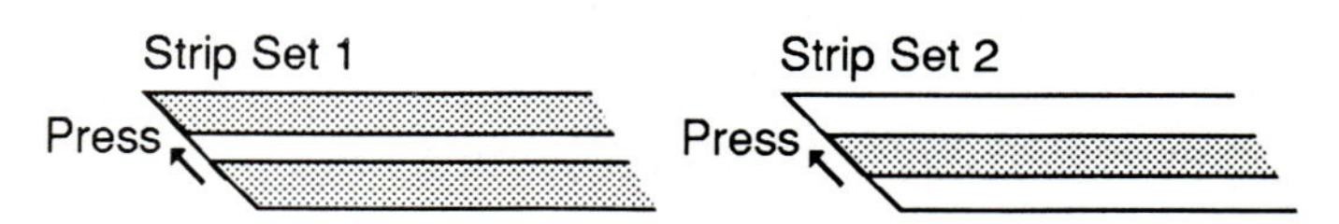

Diagram 2.

2. Sub-cut strip sections 1 and 2 at 2" intervals. Use the 45° angle on your template ruler as a guide. Make sure the 45° angle runs along the bottom edge while cutting. After cutting a couple of pieces, make sure you still have an accurate 45° angle. See Diagram 3. Cut up all the strip sections.
3. To piece the "nine-patch" diamonds follow Diagram 4. Piece 44 diamonds with a dark fabric at the point and 4 diamonds with a light fabric at the point.
4. "Proof" the diamonds by laying the template ruler over the pieced diamonds. The side angles should be 45° and the diamond should be 5" wide. See Diagram 5.

Star construction:

1. Lay out the six stars in a pleasing manner. (Refer to Whole Quilt diagram and/or picture.) Remember that one of the stars has four pieced diamonds with light points.
2. Pin and stitch two pieced diamond sections together, butting seams. See Diagram 6. Start sewing at diamond points and sew to 1/4" from bottom edge. Back stitch. Repeat for the other three pairs of diamonds. You now have four quarter sections. Press these seams so they will butt up when sections are sewn together.
3. Pin and stitch the two quarter sections together, butting seams. Remember to start sewing at the point and back stitch 1/4" from the end. You now have two halves. Press one seam in one direction and the other in the opposite direction. The top of these sections should be perfectly straight. Pin and stitch the halves together, butting seams, stopping 1/4" from end. Make all six stars. See Diagram 7.

Cutting instructions for setting fabric: (also borders and binding)

1. Cut 2 strips 10-1/4" wide. Cut 6 squares 10-1/4" x 10-1/4". Sub-cut each square diagonally in half **twice** (see diagonal sub-cutting in the General Instructions) to yield 24 inset triangles.
2. Cut 4 strips 6-7/8" wide. Cut 24 squares 6-7/8" x 6-7/8" for setting squares.
3. Cut 9 strips 2-1/4" wide for binding.
4. From remaining 2-1/4 yards, cut the strips according to Diagram 8.

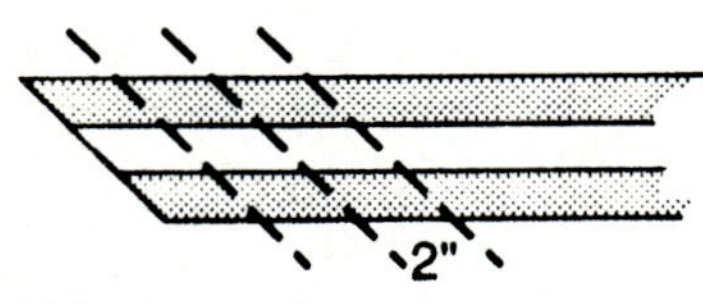

Diagram 3.

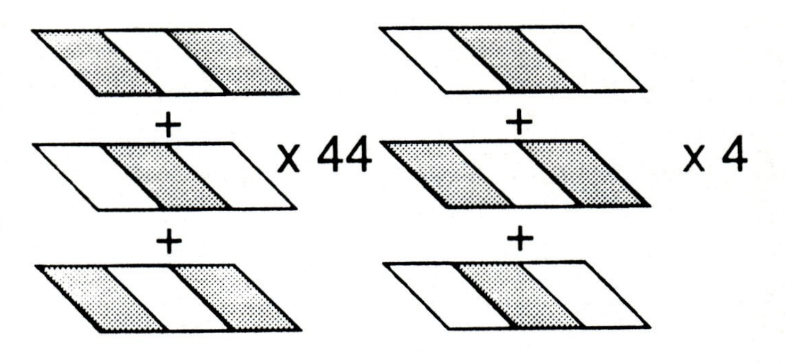

Diagram 4.

*Pin the strip sections before stitching, matching up the seamlines.

*Press the seam in the same direction on all pieces so that later the seams will butt.

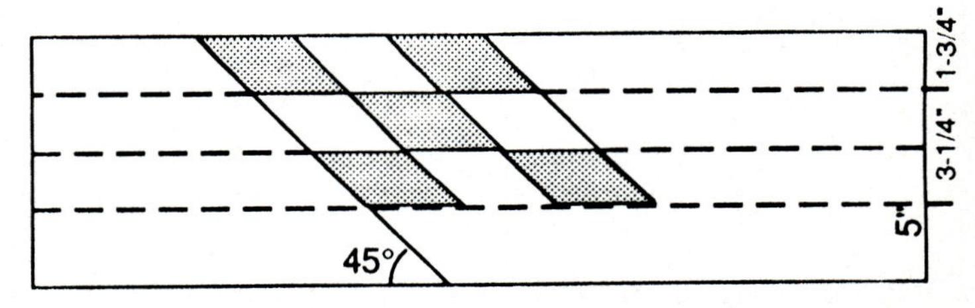

Diagram 5.

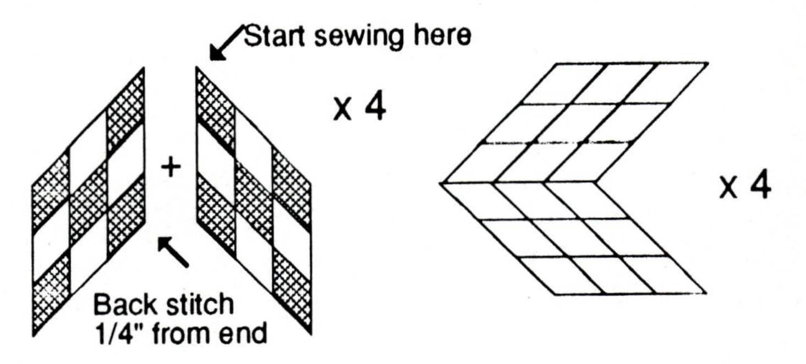

Diagram 6.

Cutting instructions for first and second borders:

1. Cut 6 strips 1-1/2" wide for the first border.
2. Cut 8 strips 2" wide for the second border.

Setting the stars:

1. Pin and sew the pre-cut corner squares (6-7/8" x 6-7/8") to the stars. You must remember to stop the stitching 1/4" in from the star. These corner squares are mitered. Press the star fabric toward the setting fabric. See Diagram 9.
2. Pin and sew the pre-cut setting triangles to the stars. Once again you must stop the stitching 1/4" in from the star. These triangles are also mitered. Press the star fabric toward the setting fabric. See Diagram 9.

Quilt layout:

1. Stitch the stars together, 2 across and 3 down. (Refer to Whole Quilt diagram)
2. Retrieve 2 of the 3-1/2" wide setting strips. Refer to "Bordering a quilt" in the General Instructions. Pin and stitch the strips to the right and left sides of the quilt.
3. Retrieve the third 3-1/2" wide strip. Piece remnants left from #2 for the top and bottom borders. Pin and stitch borders on as in #2. Press.
4. Retrieve the pre-cut first border strips (1-1/2" wide). Piece two strips together for the left border and two strips for the right border. Pin and stitch the borders on according to the General Instructions. Add the leftover strips to remaining cut strips for the top and bottom borders. Pin and stitch borders in place.
5. Retrieve the pre-cut strips (2") for the second border. Stitch two strips together for each of the four borders. Pin and stitch right and left borders to quilt as in #4. Press. Pin and stitch the top and bottom borders to quilt in same manner.

Pieced border:

1. Gather remaining strip sections left over from the stars and also the pre-cut diamond pieces. Piece borders according to whole quilt diagram. You will need four joining triangles for these borders. Cut these triangles from 2" wide pieces according to Diagram 10. The pre-sewn strip sections may be used on one side of each border, while the "loose" triangles must be pieced together for the other side.
2. Pin and stitch borders to quilt.

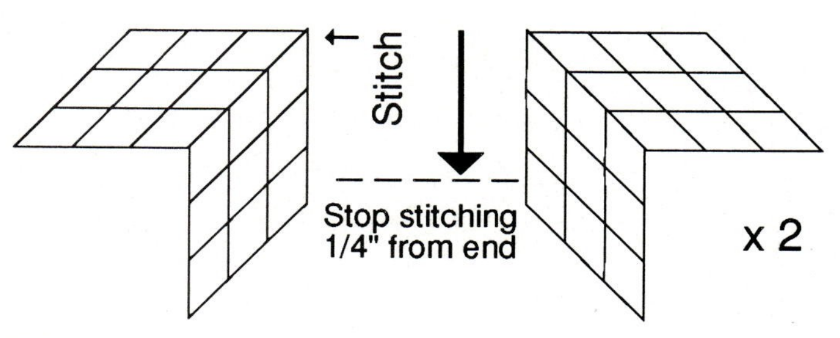

Diagram 7.

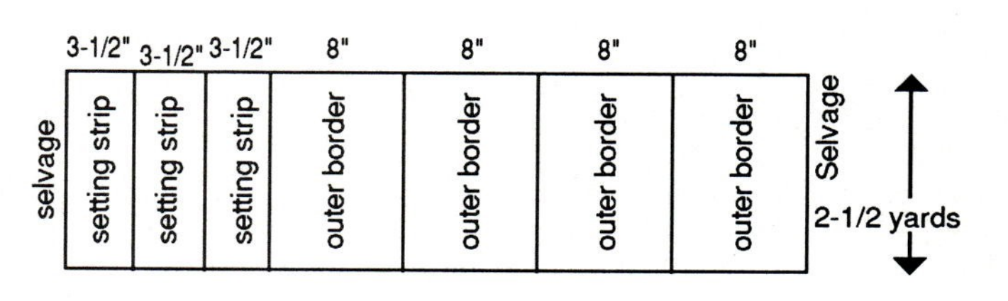

Diagram 8.

Diagram 9.

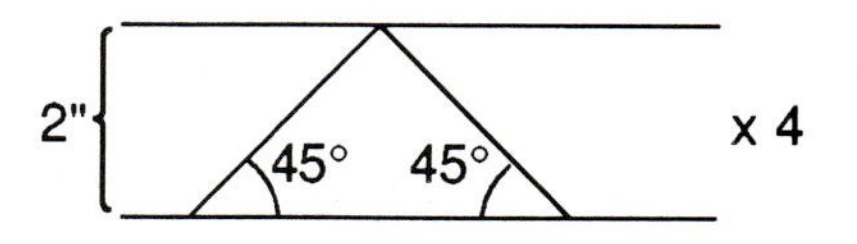

Diagram 10.

Final border:

1. Retrieve the pre-cut 8" wide border strips. Pin and stitch the right and left borders to quilt as in preceding borders. Press. Pin and stitch the top and bottom borders to the quilt.

Finishing:

1. Refer to the color picture for quilting suggestions. A purchased quilt design was used in the outer border.
2. Refer to General Instructions for layering up the quilt, hand or machine quilting, and binding your quilt.

CHERRY NUT BREAD

makes 6 4 x 6-inch loaves

1 pound margarine (softened)
1 pound confectioners' sugar (3 cups)
2 teaspoons vanilla flavoring
6 eggs
3 cups flour
2 cups chopped pecans
1 8 or 10-oz. jar of marachino cherries
— Cream margarine with sugar and vanilla. Add eggs, one at a time, and beat well after each one. Add flour one cup at a time. Mix well. Fold in nuts and chopped cherries. Mix well with a *spoon. Grease* and flour six small loaf pans 4 x 6-inch or 4 x 7-inch. Bake at 350° for 35 minutes. Test the bread to see if longer baking is required. Cool bread on wire rack. When completely cool, wrap the loaves in plastic or cellophane. Tie up with a ribbon—ready for your gift basket. Cherry nut bread also freezes well.

Scrappy Star Pillow

makes two pillows, 17-1/2" x 17-1/2"
block size: finished 14-1/2" x `4-1/2"

Pre-wash all fabrics. The scrappy stars were pieced to have a scrappy, unplanned look. Don't be afraid to use plaids, stripes, small and large scale prints. This pattern has been written for the quick-cutting and piecing methods. Please use a rotary cutter and plastic template ruler.

Fabric requirements:
— 1-1/2" wide strips of various "lights" and "darks" (10 of each)
— 5/8 yard setting fabric
— 5/8 yard backing fabric
— 5/8 yard batting
— 5/8 yard muslin
— 2 14" zippers
— 2 18" square pillow forms
— Template ruler with a 45° angle

Cutting instructions:
1. Cut 10 strips 1-1/2" wide of "dark" fabric and 10 strips 1-1/2" wide of "light" fabric. Sub-cut the strips in fourth diagonally, at a 45° angle. See Diagram 1.
2. Cut 4 strips 2" wide from the setting fabric. Cut 2 squares 7-1/4" x 7-1/4" from setting fabric. Sub-cut these squares diagonally twice for star inset triangles. ⊠
3. Cut 8 squares 4-3/4" x 4-3/4" from setting fabric for star inset corners.

Stitching strip sets:
1. Randomly pair up the cut strips into strip sets 1 and 2 as shown in Diagram 2 under Scrappy stars quilt.
2. Stitch strips sections together. They should measure 3-1/2" wide. Press all seams in one direction. Sub-cut sections 1 and 2 at 1-1/2" intervals. Use the 45° angle on your template ruler as a guide. Make sure the 45° angle runs along the bottom edge while cutting. After cutting a couple of pieces, make sure you still have an accurate 45° angle. See Diagram 2. Cut up all strip sections.
3. To piece the "nine-patch" diamonds, follow Diagram 3. Piece 16 diamonds.
4. "Proof" the diamonds by laying the template ruler over the pieced diamonds. The side angles

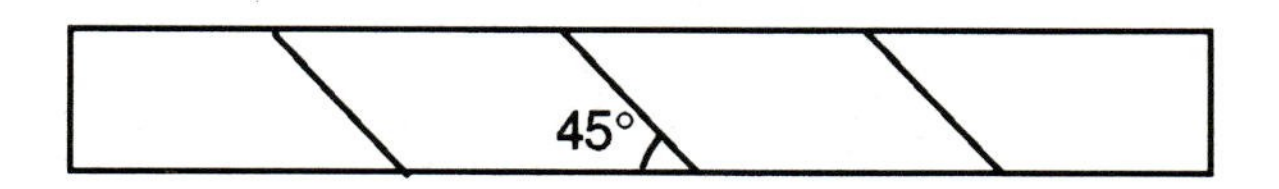

Diagram 1.

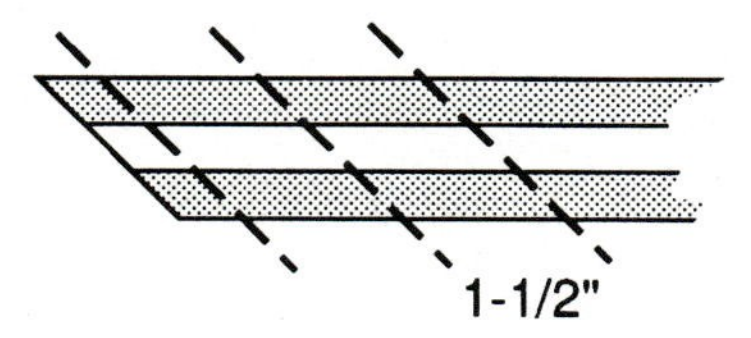

Diagram 2.

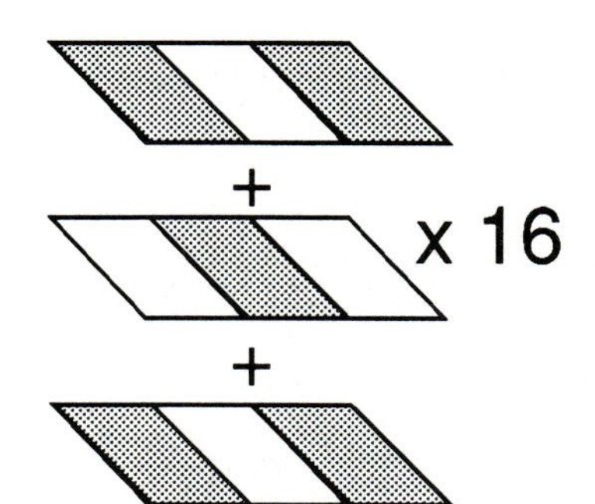

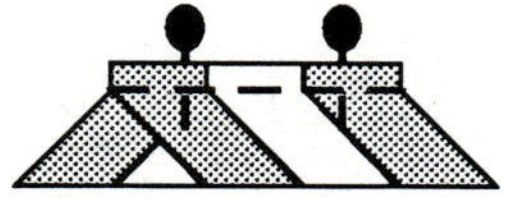

Diagram 3. **Pin the strip sections before stitching, matching up the seamlines. *Press the seam in the same direction on all pieces so that later the seams will butt.*

should be 45° and the diamond should be 3-1/2" wide. See Diagram 4.

Star construction:

1. Lay out the 2 stars in a pleasing manner.
2. Pin and stitch two pieced diamond sections together, butting seams. See Diagram 6 under Scrappy quilt. Start sewing at diamond points and sew to 1/4" from bottom edge. Back stitch. Repeat for the other three pairs of diamonds. You now have four quarter sections. Press these seams so they will butt up when sections are sewn together.
3. Pin and stitch the two quarter sections together, butting seams. Remember to start sewing at the point and back stitch 1/4" from end. You now have two halves. Press one seam in one direction and the other in the opposite direction. The top of these sections should be perfectly straight. Pin and stitch the halves together, butting seams, stopping 1/4" from end. Make both stars. See Diagram 1 under quilt.

Setting the stars:

1. Pin and stitch the pre-cut corner squares (4-3/4") to the stars. Once again you must remember to stop stitching 1/4" from the star. The corner squares are mitered. Press the star fabric towards the setting fabric.
2. Pin and stitch the pre-cut setting triangles to the stars. Once again stop stitching 1/4" in from the star. These triangles are also mitered. Press the star fabric toward the setting fabric. See Diagram 9 under Scrappy quilt.

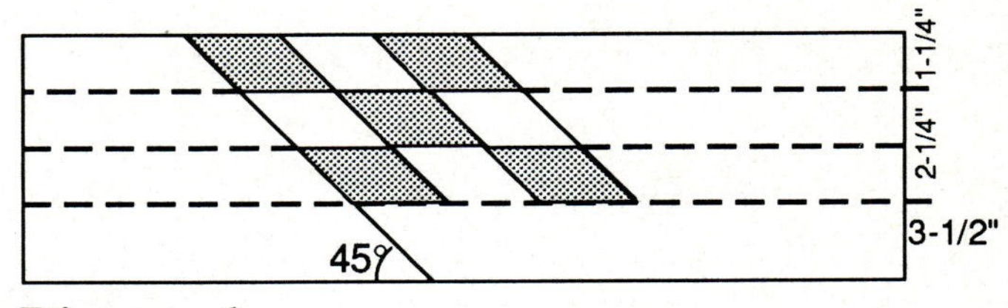

Diagram 4.

Finishing:

1. Stitch a pre-cut 2" wide strip of setting fabric to the right and left sides of star block. Press out. Stitch another setting strip to the top and bottom of block. Press out. Repeat for other block.
2. Cut a batting and muslin square a little larger than the block.
3. Refer to "Layering up a quilt" in the General Instructions. Hand or machine quilt the pillow top.
4. Refer to Log cabin pillow (under pillow construction) steps #3-7 for finishing the pillow (omit step #6.).

Template for Medallion Quilt on page 37

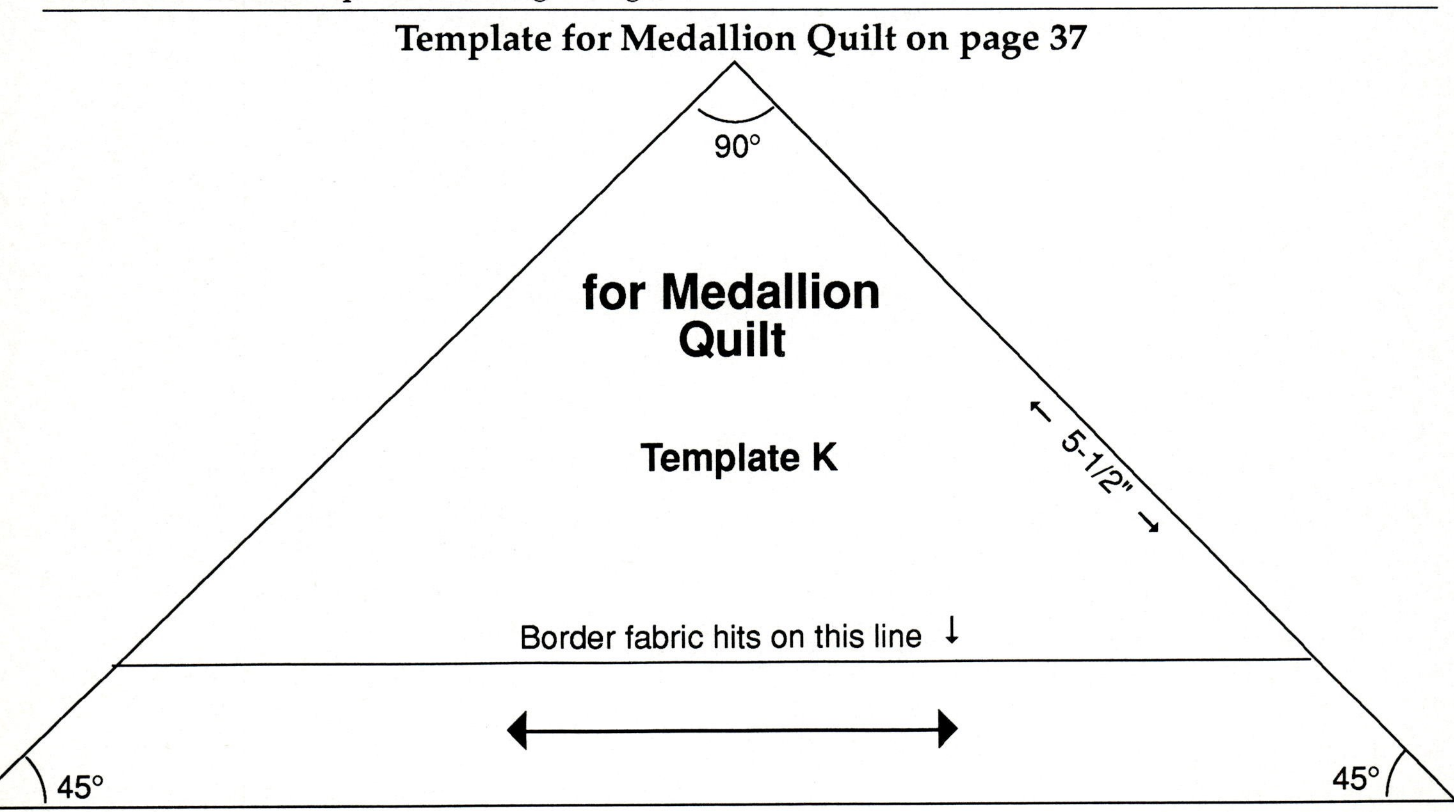

Log Cabin Pillow

finished size: 11" square

Finished size: 11" x 11"
Block size finished: 5-1/2" x 5-1/2"
Number of blocks: 4
Setting: straight

Fabric and supply requirements:
— Various light and dark fabric strips cut 1" wide
— 14" square backing fabric, batting, and muslin
— 9" zipper
—1-1/2 yards pre-gathered Kluny lace
— 11" square pillow form

Cutting instructions: (enough for 2 pillow tops, or 8 log cabin blocks)
1. From each of 10 various light value fabrics, cut 1 strip 1" wide.
2. From each of 11 various medium/dark to dark value fabrics, cut 1 strip 1" wide.
3. Cut the following logs: (for *one* log cabin block)

Dark	Light
# 1 - 1" x 1"	# 2 - 1" x 1"
# 4 - 1-1/2" x 1-1/2"	# 3 - 1" x 1-1/2"
# 5 - 1" x 2"	# 6 - 1" x 2"
# 8 - 1" x 2-1/2"	# 7 - 1" x 2-1/2"
# 9 - 1" x 3"	#10 - 1" x 3"
#12 - 1" x 3-1/2"	#11 - 1" x 3-1/2"
#13 - 1" x 4"	#14 - 1" x 4"
#16 - 1" x 4-1/2"	#15 - 1" x 4-1/2"
#17 - 1" x 5"	#18 - 1" x 5"
#20 - 1" x 5-1/2"	#19 - 1" x 5-1/2"
#21 - 1" x 6"	

4. For a greater interest, mix the order of the various fabric strips up in each block. Cut enough logs for 4 blocks.

Log Cabin construction:
1. Refer to Diagram 1 for stitching order. Stitch logs to the block in numerical order. Press after stitching each strip. Make 4 log cabin blocks.
2. Stitch the blocks together having the dark corners meet in the center of the pillow. See Diagram 2.

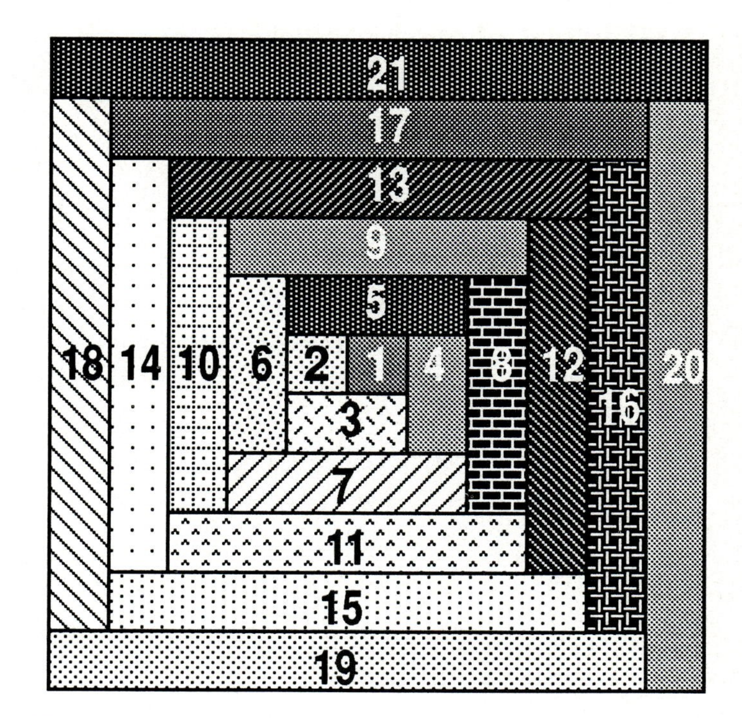

Diagram 1.

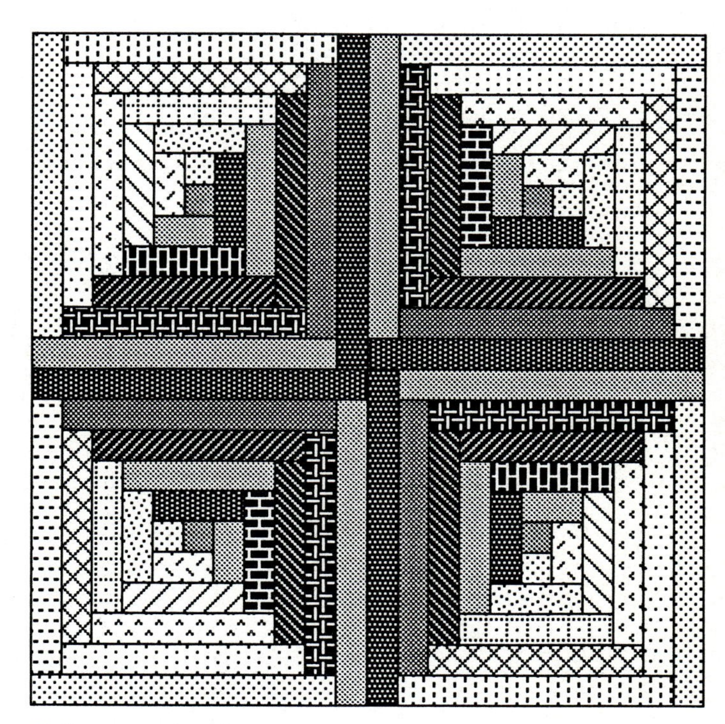

Diagram 2.

Pillow construction:

1. Retrieve the batting and muslin squares. Layer up the pillow according to the General Instructions for "Layering up a quilt".
2. Hand or machine quilt, stitch-in-a-ditch fashion. Trim excess batting and muslin.
3. Use the pillow top as a pattern for your pillow back. Cut around the sides and bottom. Remember to add 1-1/4" to the top for the zipper allowance.
4. Measure down 3" from the top and cut across, see Diagram 3. Lay these pieces right sides together. Sewing with a 5/8" seam allowance, seam 1-1/4" from each side. See Diagram 4 below. Back stitch at beginning and end. Sew with a basting stitch across the 9" opening.
5. Press seam open. Lay zipper on basted opening. Stitch zipper in, using a zipper foot. Remove basting.
6. Place a pre-gathered or flat piece of lace right sides together on pillow top. Turn raw edge of lace back 1/4" at beginning and end. Allow for extra fullness at corners. Pin. Stitch lace to pillow using 1/4" seam.
7. Open zipper a couple of inches. Place backing on pillow top, right sides together. Pin. Flip pillow over and stitch on previous stitching line. Back tack. Open zipper. Turn right sides out.
8. Make or purchase a pillow form.

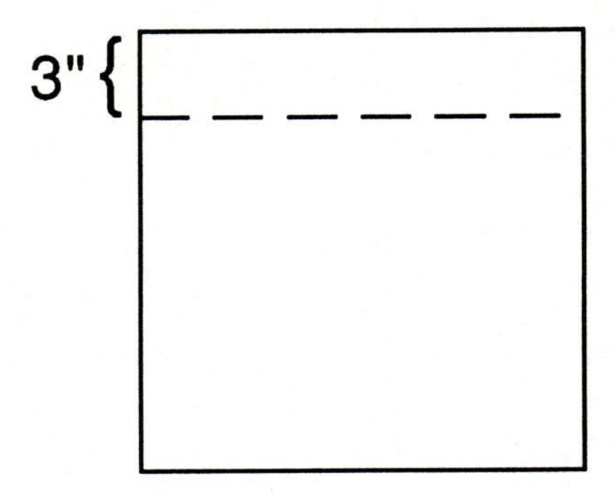

Diagram 3.

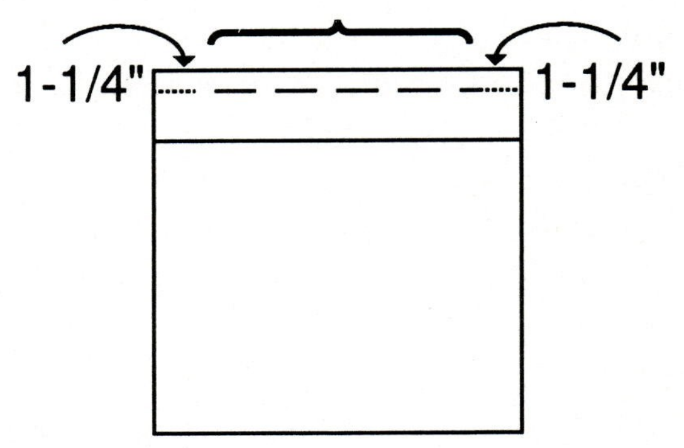

Diagram 4.

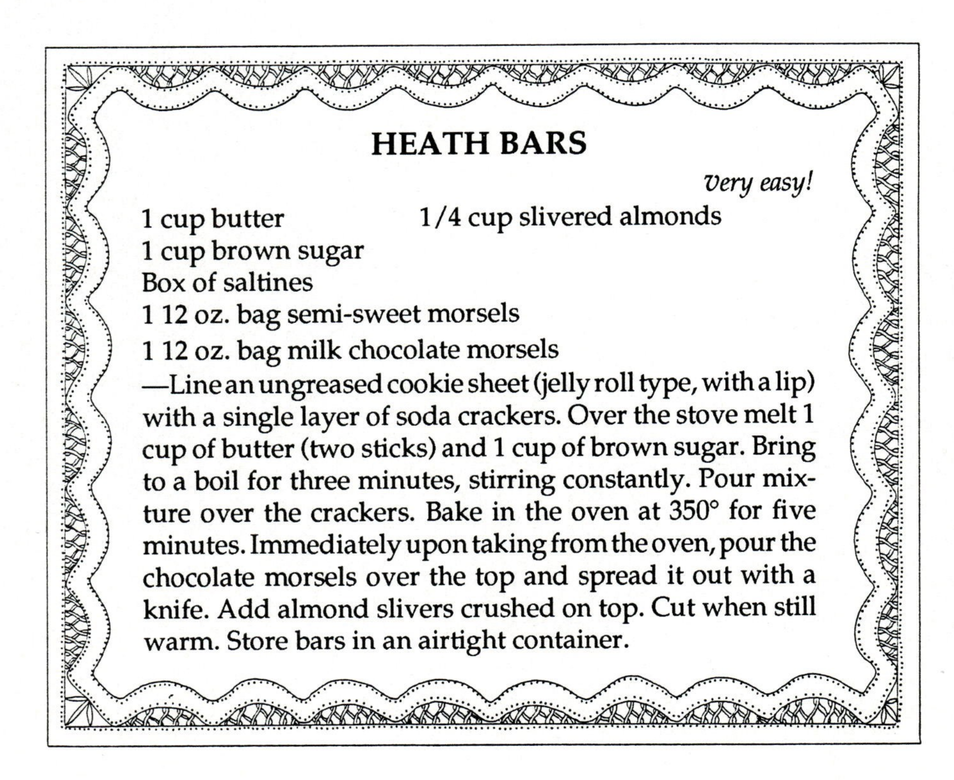

HEATH BARS

Very easy!

1 cup butter
1/4 cup slivered almonds
1 cup brown sugar
Box of saltines
1 12 oz. bag semi-sweet morsels
1 12 oz. bag milk chocolate morsels

—Line an ungreased cookie sheet (jelly roll type, with a lip) with a single layer of soda crackers. Over the stove melt 1 cup of butter (two sticks) and 1 cup of brown sugar. Bring to a boil for three minutes, stirring constantly. Pour mixture over the crackers. Bake in the oven at 350° for five minutes. Immediately upon taking from the oven, pour the chocolate morsels over the top and spread it out with a knife. Add almond slivers crushed on top. Cut when still warm. Store bars in an airtight container.

Windmill Mini-Quilt or Pillow

Quilt approximately: 15-1/2" x 15-1/2", Pillow approximately: 10" x 10"
Block size: 2-1/2" x 2-1/2" unfinished
Number of blocks: 9
Setting: diagonal

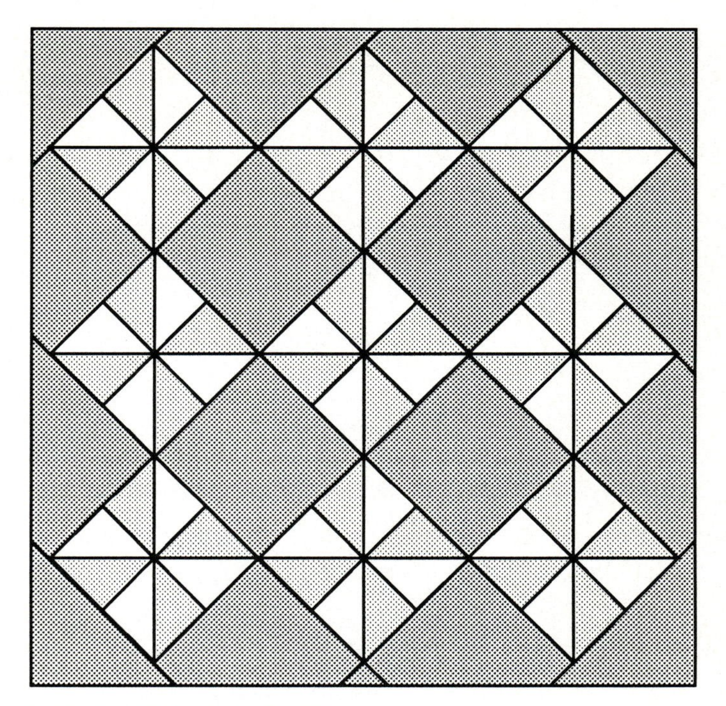

Windmill Mini-Quilt.

Pre-wash all fabrics, especially when making a pillow. The following instructions have been written for the quick-cutting method using the rotary cutter and a plastic template ruler.

Fabric requirements:
— Scraps of light, medium, medium/dark, and dark fabric
— 1/4 yard setting fabric
Additional requirements for wall quilt:
— 18" square of batting and backing
— 1/8 yard first border fabric
— 1/3 yard second border and binding fabric
Additional requirements for pillow:
— 12" square pillow backing
—13" square muslin and batting
— 9" zipper
— 1-1/2 yards 2" wide pre-gathered Kluny lace
— 10" square pillow form

Cutting instructions: (for both wallhanging and pillow top) See Diagram 1.
1. Cut 18 pieces A1 (2" x 2") from various background fabrics.
2. Cut 18 pieces A2 (2" x 2") from various darker valued fabrics.
3. Cut 1 strip 5-1/2" wide of setting fabric. Sub-cut 2 squares 5-1/2" x 5-1/2". Sub-cut these squares diagonally twice  to yield 8 triangles C. Sub-cut 2 squares 3-1/2" x 3-1/2" from the leftover strip. Sub-cut these squares in half diagonally once to yield 4 corner triangle pieces D. Sub-cut 4 squares 2-1/2" x 2-1/2" from leftover strip for pieces B.

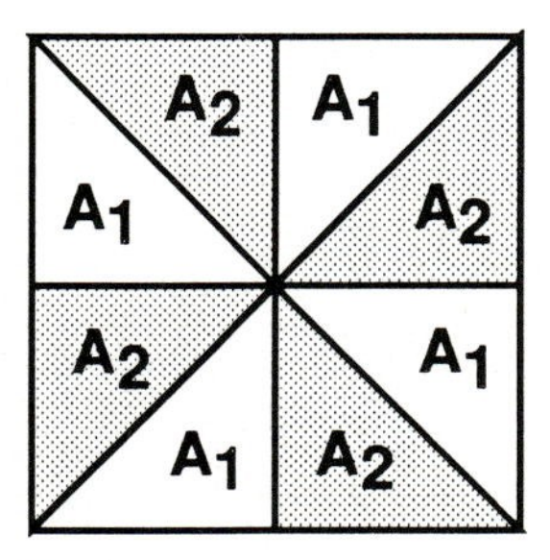

Diagram 1.

Windmill block construction:
1. Retrieve the 18 pre-cut (light) 2" squares A1. Draw a diagonal line on the wrong side of all

these squares.

2. Now pair these squares up, right sides together, with the pre-cut A2 squares.

3. Refer to the General Instructions for "Making half-square triangles". "Proof" (see General Instructions) the blocks to be 1-1/2" x 1-1/2".

4. Piece the 9 windmill blocks together according to Diagram 2. The windmill blocks should be 2-1/2" x 2-1/2" unfinished. Press in the direction of the arrows.

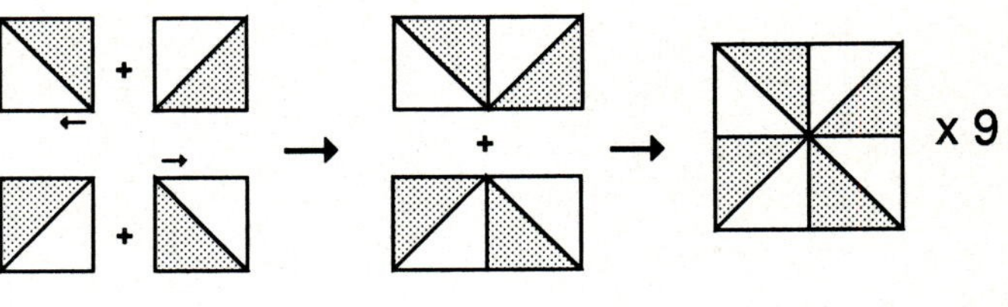

***Diagram* 2.**

Layout:

1. Retrieve all the setting pieces.

2. Follow the quilt layout Diagram 3 for piecing quilt together. The arrows show the direction for pressing. Pin and stitch row 1 to 2 to 3 to 4 to 5. Press. Pin and stitch the corners on last. "Square up" the quilt top with a 90° angle. The blocks should "float" on your setting fabric. Quilt top unfinished is approximately 10" x 10".

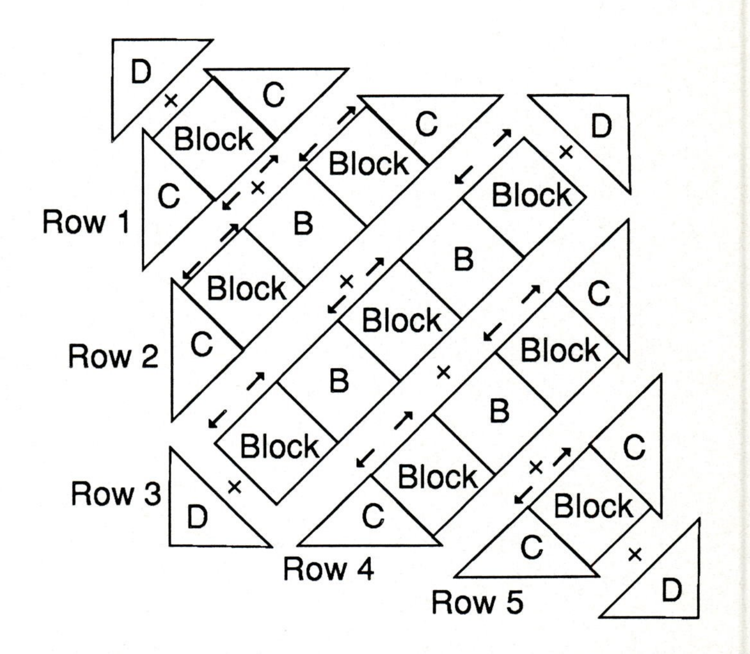

***Diagram* 3.** **Add corners last. *Press in direction of arrows.*

Windmill pillow directions:

Refer to pillow construction in Log Cabin pillow directions.

Windmill Mini quilt directions: the actual mini quilt has already been pieced

Additional cutting:

1. Cut 2 strips 1" wide for first border
2. Cut 2 strips 3" wide for second border
3. Cut 2 strips 2-1/4" wide for binding
4. Cut an 18" square from batting and backing

Finishing:

1. Measure, pin, and stitch the first and second border to quilt top according to General Instructions for "Bordering a quilt".
2. Refer to marking the quilt, layering up, machine or hand quilting, and binding for finishing the quilt in the General Instructions.

Charn Dash Mini-Quilt or Pillow

finished size: 17" x 17"
pillow: 11-1/2" x 11-1/2"

Finished size pillow: 11-1/2" x 11-1/2"
Finished size mini quilt: 17" x 17"
Block size finished: 2-1/2" x 2-1/2"
Number of blocks: 9 charn dash, 4 spacer
Setting: diagonal

Fabric requirements:
— Scraps of various light, medium, and dark value fabrics
— 1/4 yard setting (G, I, H) fabric
Continued requirements for pillow:
— 13" square of muslin and batting
— 9" zipper
— 14" square backing fabric
— 1-1/2 yards 2" wide pre-gathered Kluny lace
— 12" square pillow form
Continued requirements for mini quilt:
— 18" square of backing and batting
— 3/8 yard border and binding fabric

Cutting instructions for *one* Charn dash block: (total of 9 required) Refer to Diagram 1.
1. **From background:** cut 2 squares (2" x 2") for pieces E1 and 1 strip 1" x 6" (F1)
2. **From a dark value:** cut 2 squares (2" x 2") for pieces E2
3. **From a medium/dark fabric:** cut 1 strip 1" x 5" for F2

Cutting instructions for setting fabric (G, H, I):
1. Cut one 6" wide strip. Sub-cut into 2 squares 6" x 6". Sub-cut these squares in half diagonally twice ⊠ to yield 8 side set triangles H.
2. From the remainder of the strip, cut 2 squares 4-1/2" x 4-1/2". Sub-cut these squares in half diagonally once ⧅ to yield 4 corner triangle pieces I.
3. From the remainder of the strip cut 4 squares 3" x 3" for pieces G.

Charn Dash block construction: for **one** block
1. Retrieve the background 1" x 6" strip. Sub-cut one piece 1" x 1" for block center F1. Retrieve the other pre-cut 1" x 5" strip. Stitch these strips, right sides together, along the long edge. Press light

towards dark. Sub-cut this strip section at 1" intervals to yield 4 sections F1F2 measuring 1" x 1-1/2".

2. Retrieve the background 2" squares and the darker 2" squares. Draw a diagonal line ⍂ on the wrong side of the background squares. Place the squares right sides together. Refer to the General Instructions for "Making half-square triangles". "Proof" (refer to General Instructions for proofing) these squares to be 1-1/2" x 1-1/2".

3. Assemble the block according to Diagram 2. The arrows show pressing direction. The blocks should measure 3" x 3".

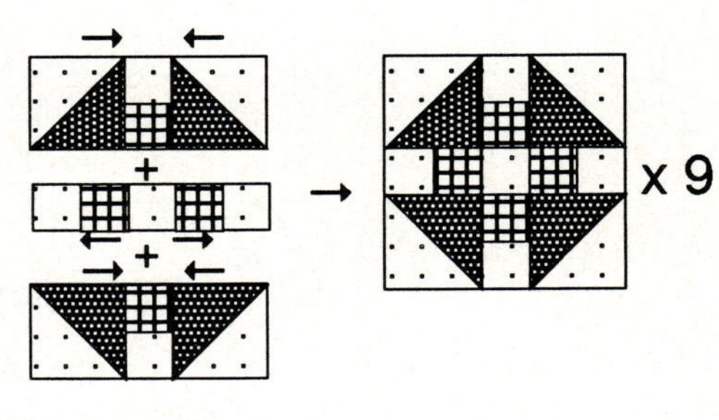

Diagram 2.

Layout:

1. Retrieve the setting pieces G, H, I.
2. Follow the layout shown in Diagram 3. The arrows show pressing direction. Pin and stitch row 1 to 2 to 3 to 4 to 5. Press. Pin and stitch the corners on last. "Square up" the quilt top with a 90° angle. The blocks should "float" on the setting fabric. Continue on to mini quilt or pillow instructions respectively.

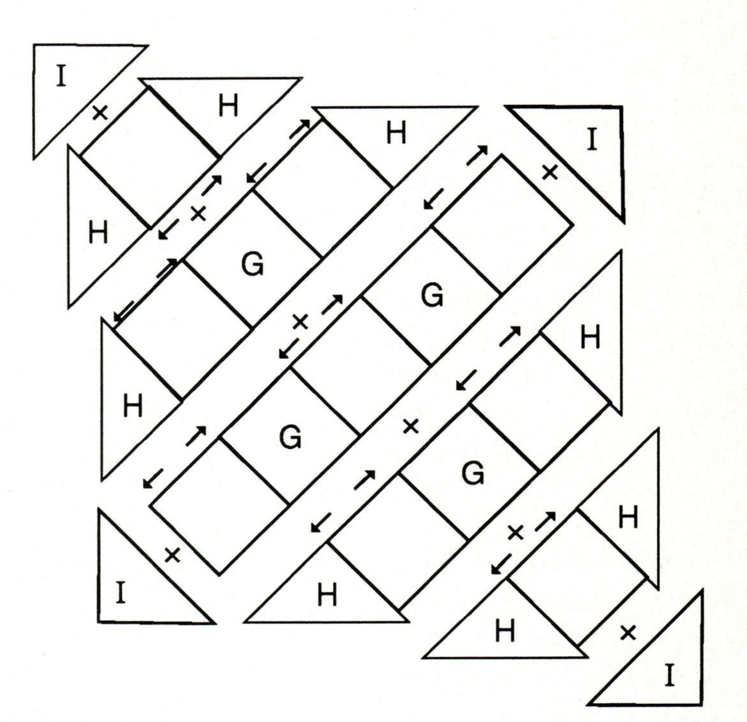

Diagram 3.

Continuation for Charn Dash Mini Quilt:
Additional cutting:
Border and binding fabric: Cut 2 strips 3" wide for border and 2 strips 2-1/4" wide for binding
Backing and batting: Cut 1 square from each 18" x 18"
Finishing: Refer to General Instructions for layering up the quilt, hand or machine quilting, and binding the quilt.

Continuation for Charn Dash Pillow:
Refer to the directions for the Log Cabin pillow under "Pillow Construction".